# YAWNING AT TIGERS

## YOU CAN'T TAME GOD, SO STOP TRYING

## DREW NATHAN DYCK

NELSON
BOOKS

An Imprint of Thomas Nelson

Published in Nashville, Tennessee, by Nelson Books, an imprint of Thomas Nelson. Nelson Books and Thomas Nelson are registered trademarks of HarperCollins Christian Publishing, Inc.

Thomas Nelson, titles may be purchased in bulk for educational, business, fundraising, or sales promotional use. For information, please e-mail SpecialMarkets@ ThomasNelson.com.

Unless otherwise indicated, Scripture quotations are taken from the Holy Bible, New International Version®, NIV®. Copyright © 1973, 1978, 1984, 2011 by Biblica, Inc.™ Used by permission of Zondervan. All rights reserved worldwide. www. zondervan.com.

Scripture quotations marked ESV are taken from THE ENGLISH STANDARD VERSION. © 2001 by Crossway Bibles, a division of Good News Publishers.

Scripture quotations marked MSG are taken from *The Message* by Eugene H. Peterson. © 1993, 1994, 1995, 1996, 2000. Used by permission of NavPress Publishing Group. All rights reserved.

Scripture quotations marked NKJV are taken from THE NEW KING JAMES VERSION. © 1982 by Thomas Nelson, Inc. Used by permission. All rights reserved.

Scripture quotations marked KJV are taken from THE KING JAMES VERSION of the Bible. Public domain.

Scripture quotations marked NLT are taken from the *Holy Bible*, New Living Translation. © 1996. Used by permission of Tyndale House Publishers, Inc., Wheaton, Illinois 60189. All rights reserved.

Scripture quotations marked RSV are taken from the REVISED STANDARD VERSION of the Bible. © 1946, 1952, 1971, 1973 by the Division of Christian Education of the National Council of the Churches of Christ in the U.S.A. Used by permission.

Italics added to Scripture quotations reflect the author's own emphasis.

Names and identifying details of some people mentioned in this book have been changed to protect their privacy.

**Library of Congress Cataloging-in-Publication Data**

Dyck, Drew.
  Yawning at tigers : you can't tame the Almighty, so stop trying / Drew Nathan Dyck.
    pages cm
  Includes bibliographical references.
  ISBN 978-1-4002-0545-5
  1. God (Christianity)--Holiness. I. Title.
  BT147.D93 2014
  231.7--dc23

                              2013042982

*Printed in the United States of America*
14 15 16 17 18 RRD 6 5 4 3 2 1

*To Dad and Mom:*

*This book is all about God.*
*Thanks for introducing us.*

# CONTENTS

# CONTENTS

# THE GREATEST ADVENTURE

**PEOPLE ARE STARVING FOR THE AWE OF GOD.**

Most don't know it, of course. They think they're starving for success or money or excitement or acceptance—you name it. But here's the problem. Even those fortunate enough to satisfy these cravings find they are still hungry. Hungrier, even.

Why? Because they've left untouched the most ancient and aching need, the one stitched into the fabric of their souls: to know and love a transcendent God.

I believe that once you strip away all our shallow desires and vain pursuits, it's God we're after. And not just any god. We have enough friends. We need a great and awesome God. A God worth worshipping.

We thirst for transcendence and long to be loved. In the full portrayal of God found in Scripture, we find both.

Our souls find satisfaction only in the God who is grand

enough to worship and close enough to love. We need a home, but we also crave adventure. The greatest adventure is to seek God.

Let it begin . . .

# PART ONE
# TIGER TERRITORY

# ONE
# DIVINE INVASION

**WE LOVE TALKING ABOUT GOD'S LOVE.**

Drop in on almost any evangelical church service and listen. You'll hear worship choruses dripping with emotive lyrics that border on romantic. The sermon will gush with assurances of God's inexhaustible affection. While such affirmations are good—we need to be reminded of God's love—something is missing. Rarely do we hear about God's mystery and majesty, let alone whisper a word about his wrath.

This one-sided portrayal diminishes our experience of God. We can't truly appreciate God's grace until we glimpse his greatness. We won't be lifted by his love until we're humbled by his holiness.

Oswald Chambers wrote, "The Bible reveals not first the love of God but the intense, blazing holiness of God."[1] This book is an invitation to encounter that blazing holiness and

3

to find, as Chambers went on to write, "his love at the center of that holiness."[2] If we long to experience that love, we must begin with a topic many of us would rather avoid: the holiness of God.

## INTO THE WILD

Tuesday, October 19, 2011, seemed like a typical day in the small town of Zanesville, Ohio. The weather was seasonably cool. It rained. People went to work. Kids went to school. And more than fifty wild animals—including lions, tigers, and bears— were loose in the area. That afternoon the 911 dispatch started receiving reports from alarmed residents: a wolf was spotted near the high school, a mountain lion on a rural road, a lion under a streetlight.

By nightfall Zanesville was in full emergency mode. Construction lights flashed the message: CAUTION: EXOTIC ANI- MALS . . . STAY IN VEHICLE. Residents were ordered indoors while local law enforcement scrambled to protect the public.

It all started when Terry Thompson, owner of a local private zoo, released his exotic animals before taking his own life. The freed animals included Bengal tigers, lions, black bears, grizzly bears, mountain lions, leopards, and wolves. "It's like Noah's ark wrecking right here in Zanesville, Ohio," said celebrity animal handler Jack Hanna.[3]

News cameras descended on Zanesville, and the world watched as the surreal event unfolded. For one evening tigers and lions stalked, not the remote jungles of Asia and Africa but the sleepy streets of suburban America. In those twilight hours, two very different worlds collided. The wild invaded the civilized. The exotic clashed with the ordinary. The familiar was disrupted by *the other.*

## YAWNING AT TIGERS

What happened in Zanesville sparked a national debate on exotic animal laws. But it led my mind in a different direction. It made me think of another unlikely encounter—not between a small town and wild animals but between humans and a holy God. Like the residents of Zanesville, we have heard reports of a foreign entity in our midst. Unlike them, however, we often fail to appreciate the gravity of what that presence means.

The Bible describes God in sobering terms. Among the myriad titles given, he is called "a consuming fire," "Judge of all the earth," and the "Lord of hosts"[4]—a title that portrays God poised for battle, at the head of a heavenly army. In addition to these fearsome descriptions, the Bible stresses God's discontinuity with humankind. "God is not human, that he should . . ." is almost a refrain in Scripture.[5] We might imagine that God is a sort of Superman, just like you or me but with additional powers. But that kind of thinking betrays a dangerous illusion about God's nature. The truth is that God is radically different from us, in degree and kind. He is ontologically dissimilar, wholly other, dangerous, alien, holy, and wild.

If we truly believed this kind of God was in our midst, I wonder if we would respond more like the people in Zanesville— lock our doors and call the police.

But for the most part we neither tremble in fear nor thrill

with excitement at the prospect of encountering this wild deity. Instead our church experiences are largely predictable and sedate. Our spiritual lives are devoid of passion. Yes, we believe, but often our knowledge of God is dry and cerebral. We give mere mental assent to truths that should leave us shaking. We mumble perfunctory prayers. We ask God to keep us safe, not realizing that it is from him we most need protecting. Even when we see evidence of God in our midst, when we glimpse his holiness, we're more likely to yawn than yell. Somehow we've succeeded in making the strange ordinary. We walk by tigers without looking twice.

Why are we so anesthetized? What's behind our lack of reverence, fear, and awe?

I think it's simple.

We've forgotten how big God is.

## DANGEROUS PRESENCE

I remember having this point presented in dramatic fashion when I visited Israel. I was there with a group of American journalists. Our Jewish guide, Amir, had been leading trips through the Holy Land for thirty years and had a profound grasp of Scripture. At each site we visited, Amir would seek out a spot as isolated as possible from the never-ending stream of tourists, gather us in a semicircle, and expound upon the historical and theological significance of the site. Sometimes he seemed more like a preacher than a tour guide. I remember one talk in particular. With the Mount of Olives shimmering in the background, Amir described what he saw as the basic problem of the universe.

"God longs to come down to earth to redeem the righteous and judge the wicked," he said. "But there's a problem."

He leaned toward us and stretched out his arms like a scarecrow.

"His presence is like radiation, more dangerous than plutonium. Nothing can live when God comes near. If God came to earth, both the righteous and unrighteous would perish. It would be like a thousand nuclear bombs exploding at once. We would all die!"

Initially Amir's God-as-plutonium metaphor struck me as strange. I've heard God described as a father, master, king, warrior, judge . . . but plutonium? Plutonium is pretty nasty stuff. Actually, it's awful. If inhaled, it's one of the deadliest elements known to man. Other kinds of radiation, like an X-ray, the body can handle in low dosages. But just one-millionth of a gram of plutonium will kill a person if it enters the lungs. One pound could kill millions.[6]

I remember watching the news in the wake of the scramble to contain the Fukushima Daiichi nuclear plant disaster in Japan in 2011. An article in the *Wall Street Journal* described the precautions taken by the emergency workers. In addition to constantly measuring radiation with cell-phone-sized dosimeters strapped to their chests, they wore "face masks with two filters . . . hooded Tyvek suits, three layers of gloves and covers for their shoes. They wound tape at sleeves and pants cuffs to seal gaps."[7] Even these precautions were decried by experts as too lax. That's how dangerous plutonium is—when it gets out.

## OTHER AND INTIMATE

Amir's comparison seemed strange, maybe even sacrilegious. But as I recounted God's interactions with the ancient Israelites, I wondered if Amir was onto something.

I thought of all the stories surrounding the ark of the covenant, where people were struck dead or sickened from coming in contact with God's immediate presence. I thought of poor Uzzah, the Israelite who was killed for putting out his hand to steady the ark of the covenant (2 Sam. 6:7). Or the times when God warned Moses to keep the people back from his glory lest God "break out against them" (Ex. 19:22). In these stories it almost seems like there was some kind of radioactive field surrounding God. Not literally, perhaps, but from reading these accounts you get the unmistakable idea that his holiness is dangerous, even deadly.

We tend to avoid these passages or explain them away. Each time a popular atheist writes a book accusing God of being mean (and somehow simultaneously nonexistent), we spill gallons of ink trying to defend God's actions. While I appreciate the works of apologists, this sort of enterprise often becomes a subtle way of domesticating God. After we get through explaining him, he comes off as misunderstood or hapless. I'd prefer to say, "Yes, God is dangerous. He's not a house cat; he's a lion. You're free to deny his existence or pretend that he's harmless. Go ahead and pet him if you'd like; just don't expect to get your arm back."

I'm reminded of the sad, strange story of Ellie Quo, a thirty-two-year-old Australian man who decided to put his fighting skills to the ultimate test. In the spring of 1989, after being told by his kung fu instructor that he had reached a level where he could kill wild animals with his bare hands, the impressionable student decided it was time to take on the most lethal predator. He sneaked into the Melbourne Zoo at night and scaled the lion enclosure. But rather than doing battle with one lion, he faced several. The fight ended with predictable results, and zookeepers found Quo (or what was left of him) the next morning.[8]

It's a bizarre story that makes you question Quo's sanity. How could anyone, regardless of training, hope to take on a pack of lions with his or her bare hands? Yet the ill-fated man's foolishness is nothing compared to mere mortals who claim parity with an omnipotent God.

Perhaps it was to convey this dangerous side of God that pastor and author Eugene Peterson half-jokingly suggested churches post signs outside their buildings that read: BEWARE THE GOD.[9]

"The places and occasions that people gather to attend to God are dangerous," Peterson explains. "They're glorious places and occasions, true, but they're also dangerous. Danger signs should be conspicuously placed, as they are at nuclear power stations."[10]

Pulitzer-prize-winning writer Annie Dillard takes it a step further:

> On the whole, I do not find Christians, outside the catacombs, sufficiently sensible of the conditions. Does anyone have the foggiest idea what sort of power we so blithely invoke? Or, as I suspect, does no one believe a word of it? The churches are children playing on the floor with their chemistry sets, mixing up a batch of TNT to kill a Sunday morning. It is madness to wear ladies' straw hats and velvet hats to church; we should all be wearing crash helmets. Ushers should issue

life preservers and signal flares; they should lash us to our pews. For the sleeping god may wake someday and take offense, or the waking god may draw us out to where we can never return.[11]

Such vivid warnings may sound like exaggeration, but are they? Each year four or five people die at the Grand Canyon because of "overly zealous photographic endeavors."[12] In search of the perfect picture, these tourists disregard warning signs and venture too close to the precipice. They underestimate the risk and end up paying the ultimate price. When we approach God casually, as if he were some sort of cosmic buddy, we make a similar mistake. We demonstrate a dangerous misunderstanding about his nature.

Don't get me wrong. God is not cruel and capricious. But Amir was right—he's dangerous. And that presents us with a huge problem. God's holiness is deadly, incompatible with life, especially for sinful mortals like us. "No one may see me," God warned, "and live" (Ex. 33:20).

But so far I've been telling only half of the story. Because just when God's holiness seems overwhelming, when the gulf between us seems hopelessly wide, that's where the gospel comes in. The good news is that this dangerous God turns out to be a lover. And he's not content to love us from a distance. He wants to be with us so desperately he cooked up the most creative and costly way imaginable to bridge the chasm.

God is dangerous, yes, but loving. He's above and beyond our physical world, yet mysteriously present within it. This, of course, is the grand paradox of the Christian faith. We worship a God transcendent and immanent, other and intimate, high and lifted up yet closer than our own breath.

He's the Intimate Stranger, and we are the objects of his fierce affection. Now the temple veil is torn. The Holy of Holies beckons, and we're free to enter. Just remember to tread lightly . . . he's still the same God.

## TWO
# BEYOND THE SHALLOWS

**MY WIFE AND I RECENTLY CELEBRATED OUR TEN-YEAR** anniversary in Kona, Hawaii. It was an incredible trip, though not your typical romantic getaway. The reason? We brought along our eight-month-old son.

It's amazing how many things you *can't* do on the Big Island with a baby in tow. No surfing, no snorkeling, no kayaking, no crater climbing, no late-night luaus. More than once we wondered aloud whether we should have made the trip with such a young child. But by the end, we were glad we did. There's nothing quite like watching a child watch the world. And when that world is filled with the vivid sights of a tropical paradise, it's even better.

On one of our first evenings there, while my wife was getting ready to go out for dinner, I walked our son down to the beach. The early months of his life had passed in the landlocked Midwest, so this would be his first glimpse of the ocean.

As we neared the water's edge, I was curious to see his reaction. Would he smile? Giggle? Open his mouth and unleash one of his familiar "Gee, gee, gee!" exclamations? Or stare, awestruck?

He cried.

I should have anticipated his response. The tide was in. The waves were high. They sped toward us with a growing roar before slamming into the rocky shoreline, churning up stones, and spewing them across the pebbled beach. It was a violent scene.

As my son took it all in, his bottom lip started to tremble. Then he jerked his head from the sight and stifled a scream against my shoulder. Suddenly I understood how strange and terrifying the pounding waves must have appeared to him. He'd never seen anything like it. What guarantee did he have that the next angry surge would stop before swallowing us whole?

His reaction made perfect sense: the ocean is overwhelming. And not just for children. Truth be told, I'm a little scared of it too. Poets wax eloquently about the ocean's beauty, its power to inspire serenity and introspection—and that's all true. But there's another side to the sea, a scary side, the side of powerful tempests and deadly creatures and dark depths. There's a reason swimming instructors tell you to respect the ocean. If you don't, it can kill you.

When I was about twelve years old, I remember looking out over the ocean at night and trying to imagine what it would be like to swim out into those black waters. It was about the scariest thought I'd ever entertained.

Vast, beautiful, powerful, dangerous—that's the ocean. It makes me think of God, which is probably appropriate. Both are immense, mysterious. Both can make us feel frighteningly small. The appropriate response to such greatness is respect and awe, even resignation. Yet often we tend to do something else, something very strange. We devise ways to make them more manageable. We scale them down to our size. We domesticate them. Or at least we try.

## THE LURE OF LESSER GODS

This impulse is nothing new. It's been around for millennia.

Ancient Israel is Exhibit A. I'm stunned by how often the Israelites turned their backs on God to worship more manageable deities. We read about one such instance in Exodus 32. The story unfolds as Moses was on Mount Sinai receiving the Ten Commandments. Frustrated by their leader's extended absence, the Israelites approached Aaron, the second-in-command, with a request: "Come, make us gods who will go before us" (v. 1).

Aaron obliged and got to work. Gold jewelry was collected and melted down. Then Aaron formed the gold into "an idol cast in the shape of a calf" (v. 4). The next day the Israelites rose early to make sacrifices to the golden calf.

This act of idolatry seems to come out of the blue. The Lord had just dramatically rescued the Israelites from slavery and supernaturally sustained them in the wilderness. It was only "the third month," we're told, since they had been liberated from Egypt (Ex. 19:1). That means the Red Sea parting was still vivid in their minds; the taste of manna clung to their breath. They'd drunk water from a rock and been guided by a cloud and a pillar of fire. Yet after witnessing these miracles and receiving repeated assurances of God's protection and provision, they chose to worship an idol instead.

What was going on? Throughout history, people have struggled to understand this abrupt descent into idolatry. The early church leader Origen was puzzled by how a people so quickly could have "forgotten the benefits and marvels performed by God."[1] The sixteenth-century theologian John Calvin, too, was baffled. "Could they not see the pillar of fire and the cloud?" he asked. "Was not God's paternal solicitude abundantly conspicuous every day in the manna? Was He not near them in ways innumerable?"[2] We might echo this bewilderment in more contemporary language: *What were they thinking? How could anyone encounter the living God one day and bow before an idol the next?*

The answer isn't clear. It is possible the Israelites were simply slipping back into the practices of their Egyptian captors. The ancient Near East was brimming with idols, so idolatry was the default religious practice of the day. With their leader taking his sweet time on the mountain, the Israelites became restless and scared—and they turned back to what was most familiar. The early church historian Eusebius wrote that the Israelites were "trained" in idolatry by four hundred years of slavery under the idol-worshipping Egyptians.[3] Reverting to idol worship was natural because of such ingrained habits.

But I think more than bad habits were at work here. Forty days before the golden-calf incident, the Israelites witnessed an awesome spectacle. The Lord told Moses that he was going to descend upon the mountain "in a dense cloud" and instructed Moses to consecrate the people for the occasion (Ex. 19:9–10). After three days of purification rituals, the Lord showed up.

On the morning of the third day there was thunder and lightning, with a thick cloud over the mountain, and a very loud trumpet blast. Everyone in the camp trembled. Then Moses led the people out of the camp to meet with God, and they stood at the foot of the mountain. Mount Sinai was covered with smoke, because the LORD descended on it in fire. The smoke billowed up from it like smoke from a furnace, and the whole mountain trembled violently. . . . The sound of the trumpet grew louder and louder. (Ex. 19:16–19)

It's a powerful scene, one that underscores God's holiness and majesty. It's also absolutely terrifying. After such an overwhelming encounter, I wonder if the idea of a mute idol seemed strangely attractive—for comfort if nothing else.

Here, the contrast between God and an idol couldn't be clearer. We're told that after offering sacrifices to the golden calf, the Israelites "sat down to eat and drink and got up to indulge in revelry" (Ex. 32:6). But when God descended on Mount Sinai, "everyone in the camp trembled" (Ex. 19:16). You don't tremble before an idol.

You can see an idol. It's visible, tangible. Yahweh, on the other hand, is invisible and forbids representation. And just in case you felt like making a run for the mountain to steal a glimpse of his glory, there's this: "Warn the people," God told Moses, "so they do not force their way through to see the LORD and many of them perish" (Ex. 19:21).

The differences don't stop there. You can also control an idol. You determine everything about it: what it's made out of, where it goes, and how it's worshipped. Not so with the sovereign Creator of heaven and earth, who alone dictates the terms of his worship.

An idol is safe. It never challenges you. It isn't threatening. It doesn't judge sin or demand loyalty. But the Holy One of Israel is a jealous God—passionate and loving, yes, but unspeakably dangerous too.

The actions of the Israelites might seem strange to us, but when you consider the challenges of worshipping the living God, the lure of tame idols makes much more sense.

Are we all that different from the Israelites? We may not melt down jewelry to make golden calves, but we're continually pulling God down to our level. We're forever creating more comfortable versions of him to worship. We, too, exchange intimacy with the living God for "the dangerous illusion of a manageable deity."[4]

I think it's interesting that after casting the idol, Aaron proclaimed, "These are your gods, Israel, who brought you up out of Egypt" (Ex. 32:4). Then he announced to the people, "Tomorrow there will be a festival to the Lord" (v. 5).

Those gods didn't bring them out of Egypt. And how could an idolatrous party be described as a "festival to the Lord"? Many believe that the idol (or idols) Aaron fashioned may have actually been intended to represent Yahweh. If that was the case, the great sin of the Israelites at Sinai was not worshipping other gods. It was assigning God a replacement. It was reducing God to something he is not and making that the object of worship. In other words, it was something we do all the time.


## THE GOD LAGOON


One of the highlights of our anniversary trip to Hawaii was staying in the Hilton Waikoloa Village, a sprawling four-star resort located on the Kohala Coast of the Big Island. We could only afford to stay there two nights, but it was worth the price. We didn't even have to leave the 62-acre, 1,240-room resort to have a good time. It featured a dozen restaurants and a variety of shops, boutiques, and galleries. In the daytime we swam in the pools and dined in the open-air restaurants. In the evenings we strolled the meticulously gardened grounds, taking in the lush vegetation and cascade waterfalls. When our feet got tired or the baby got fussy, we simply hopped on the air-conditioned tram that whisked us back to our room.

But the big draw for us was the lagoon, an enclosure the resort's website described as "teeming with tropical fish and rare green sea turtles . . . a protected oasis perfect for snorkeling and swimming."[5] The lagoon, of course, was man-made. Every minute ten thousand gallons of water were pumped in from the ocean. All dangerous marine life was screened out. There were no jellyfish or barracudas or sharks in the lagoon. Nothing with stingers or poison or fangs. No spiny backs or razor teeth. Just slow-swimming turtles and brightly colored fish. Beside the lagoon was a perfectly rectangular, white-sand beach with cabanas for rent. And yes, the Lagoon Grill to fill you up between swims.

After getting situated on the beach, my wife and I took turns swimming while the other parent watched the baby. I jumped into the water first and swam for the other side. The water wasn't perfectly clear, but I made out several large fish passing beneath me. When I reached the rocks on the far side, I even spotted a sea turtle. I swam back to the beach, toweled off, and it was my wife's turn.

The lagoon was enjoyable (it definitely beat a cold night in

Chicago), but after an hour or so something unforeseen happened. We got bored.

Why did the initial thrill of crisscrossing the enclosure fade so quickly? Maybe we had unrealistic expectations. I had been attracted by the promise of an authentic marine adventure, but this felt more like swimming in a large pool stocked with fish and turtles. Perhaps the experience was diminished by the fact that the lagoon was crowded with other vacationers, many riding inner tubes, paddleboats, canoes, and giant water bicycles.

But the problem really wasn't what was in the lagoon. It's what wasn't. There were no waves, no spray from the surf, no tides, no coral reefs, no danger, no depths.

It wasn't the ocean.

At one point I looked over my shoulder at the sea. It lay about a hundred feet away and seemed to stretch forever beyond the horizon. "You know," I said to my wife, "we could swim in there."

I believe there's a spiritual equivalent to that man-made lagoon. If the ocean is like God, the lagoon is a poor, but useful, replacement. It's domesticated Christianity. It's engagement with a lesser deity. It's the golden calf in place of Yahweh. It's a life designed to give us spiritual experiences while cushioning us from the reality of a dangerous God.

Just like the man-made lagoon had real ocean water and marine life, this "god lagoon" may contain some spiritual truths. We may even encounter qualities of the true God—but only the ones we deem acceptable. Divine characteristics we find threatening or that clash with our modern sensibilities, we carefully screen out. Life in the lagoon means never being surprised by God. It means never having to take seriously what he might have us do or ask us to give up. Ultimately, it means we are in control.

The power of the god lagoon lies in its subtlety. It's easy to think you're in the ocean when you're immersed in saltwater and surrounded by sea turtles. And it's easy to believe we're encountering God because we go to church, sing the songs, pray the prayers, and interact with Christians. But we can do all those things without ever having to grapple with the real presence of God.

And it's not like the lagoon is filled with pagans and heretics. It's filled with us—well-meaning believers who gladly pay lip service to the central doctrines of the Christian faith. But here's the rub. Somewhere along the line we've distanced ourselves from those truths. We haven't let them, or the God who revealed them, invade our reality. In a thousand little ways, we've chosen the comfort of the shallows over life in the deep.

Of course it's natural to ask, if the lagoon is so comfortable, why leave? Why not remain ensconced in its safe, warm waters? Well, for the same reason my wife and I were disappointed by that resort lagoon. It's not real. And it gets boring. Sure, it's fun for a while. But it's not invigorating. One day you wade in and realize you've been splashing around in a bounded enclosure of your own imagining. And there's something inside you that longs to leave the lagoon and strike out for the deep.

So many of us live what one writer called "lives of quiet desperation."[6] We're bored to death of living but scared to death to really live. What if what's really missing are the deep things of God? What if it's not that next accomplishment or superficial thrill? What if only a ravishing vision of God's grandeur will make the difference? Maybe that's what it takes to make you want to crawl back into your life. Maybe only the deep will do.

## EYE-POPPING BEAUTY

What is the deep? It's where we encounter God. Not God as we might imagine him to be, but God how he really is. How he has revealed himself to us.

We might not always like what we find in the deep. We will likely discover truths that make us uncomfortable or even offend us. We should never expect eternal truth to neatly fulfill our twenty-first-century expectations. Nor can we demand safety there.

Poet John Blase writes a reflection in which he invites readers to leave the shallows to follow Jesus out into the deep. But he offers this caveat:

> Now in the interest of full disclosure I should mention that out there in the deep you might drown, or get eaten by a shark, or get a charley horse then flail around thus drawing the attention of leviathan. The only guarantee is God's presence. That's the deal. That's the deep.[7]

Of course he's right. Life in the deep is dangerous because it's life with God. So why risk it? Because there isn't just danger in the deep; there's wonder too.

Again, consider the ocean.

In 2010, after a decade of work by nearly three thousand researchers, scientists produced the first Census of Marine Life. The researchers discovered six thousand new species, bringing the total number of known marine species to two hundred and fifty thousand.

Highlights from the study ranged from the bizarre to the beautiful: six-hundred-year-old tube worms, herring that swim in formations as large as Manhattan, the yeti crab with long, downy claws, a jellyfish with a Darth Vader–like helmet, and another jellyfish that uses lights to "scream" for help.

One of the leaders for the project said, "Life astonished us everywhere we looked. . . . The discoveries of new species and habitats both advanced science and inspired artists with their extraordinary beauty." Another scientist who participated in the research effused, "The most surprising thing was the beauty. . . . Our eyes were popping out of our heads."[8]

That's the kind of beauty that's worth searching for. And it's a mere glimpse of the wonders awaiting us in the depths of God. To communicate something of the boundless nature of God, the apostle Paul turned to poetry:

> *Oh, the depth of the riches of the wisdom and knowledge of God!*
> *How unsearchable his judgments,*
> *and his paths beyond tracing out!*
> *"Who has known the mind of the Lord?*
> *Or who has been his counselor?"*
> *"Who has ever given to God,*
> *that God should repay them?" (Rom. 11:33–35)*

We will never plumb the depths of God. Yet I'm amazed by how much God has chosen to reveal to us. Paul also wrote that we have received God's Spirit, who "searches all things, even the deep things of God" (1 Cor. 2:10).

If we have access to the deep things of God, why would we ever be bored? Why are we so often spiritually complacent? I don't think it's because we lack faith or are more sinful than anyone else. And it's certainly not because God is boring. But over the years, we slowly lose sight of how strange and splendid God truly is. My friend Margaret Feinberg wrote about this tendency:

> Many of us say we want to experience God, but we don't look for his majesty. We travel life's paths with our heads down, focused on the next step with our careers or families or retirement plans. But we don't really expect God to show up with divine wonder.[9]

Slowly, subtly, God becomes ordinary, commonplace. As our view of his grandeur dims, our spiritual lives become dull. Instead of striking off for the depths, we never leave the beach. We're like marine researchers, equipped with all the tools and resources to explore the deepest fathoms of the sea, who instead opt to build sandcastles on the shore.

Speaking of the sea, something strange happened the next time my son saw it.

The day after swimming in the resort we went down to the water again. Not to the man-made lagoon but to the wild sea itself. This time my son's reaction was different. Rather than turning in fear from the pounding waves, he was mesmerized. Craning his neck to see past me, he looked out at the majestic swells.

He wouldn't stop staring.

# THREE
# THE GOD WORTH WORSHIPPING

**AS TWENTYSOMETHINGS, MY WIFE AND I WERE NOMADS.**
Every few years we would pack up our Volkswagen Beetle and strike out for new jobs or further education. The transience meant finding churches to attend in a variety of cities, including Portland, Los Angeles, Orlando, and Chicago.

Typically we'd start with a megachurch. Even when you're new to a city, they aren't hard to find. We could slip into these behemoths late (no one seemed to mind) and settle into padded theater seats in the balcony. The messages were always excellent, if sometimes a little short on substance, and the music was professional-grade. But what we found most attractive about these churches, honestly, was the anonymity. Small churches are intensely interpersonal. You can't attend a service at a small church (or skip one) without being noticed. The megachurch experience couldn't be more different. You can come and go like a ghost. For two twentysomethings who knew they weren't going to be in town long, that was a draw.

The next type of church we tried was what I called the warehouse church, so named because they were held in settings designed to look like warehouses. Think Urban Outfitters—high ceilings, cement floors, exposed ductwork—but with stackable chairs and candles. These services were filled with other twentysomethings, and whoever organized them seemed to be reading from the same script. The rooms were dimly lit with large projection screens that stretched skyward over a small band of hip musicians. Couches would be arranged in circles near the back of the room to facilitate prayer and discussion. It felt like something between a church service and a coffee-shop poetry reading. After an extended time of singing, a stylish, young guy would amble to the front of the room, sit on a stool, and talk earnestly about his spiritual experiences, glancing down occasionally at notes on a mobile device. These services were usually held in the basements of larger churches. I learned later that most were part of a broader strategy. The services were engineered as incubators for young people. When the attendees were old enough, it was assumed we'd join everyone else in "big church."

We also tried a couple of mainline churches. Since my wife and I had both grown up in Low Church settings, we figured we could use a little tradition. But in these churches we found the theology wanting. I remember one sermon in particular. It had a certain lyrical elegance. The pastor spent forty minutes effusing about love in abstract terms, yet there was scant engagement with Scripture. In fact, there was nothing distinctly Christian about the message. We might as well have been at a Kiwanis Club meeting or a charity pledge drive.

Finally we settled in community churches, usually nondenominational. We liked the fact that they weren't comprised solely of people our age. There were soccer moms and seniors, city dwellers and suburbanites, families and singles. And we liked that they took the Bible seriously, at least in theory. Still, the sermons were heavy on self-help and light on substance: "How to Have a Good Family," "How to Overcome Anger," "How to Build a Better Marriage," and so on.

Not that my wife and I didn't learn and grow participating in the life of these communities. We had rich times of fellowship. We worshipped and served and forged friendships. Just as we were getting involved, it seemed it was time to load up the Beetle again and aim for a new point on the map. The transience, however, gave us a unique perspective. In the space of four years we lived in as many cities and attended even more churches, sampling the spectrum.

During that time I had a growing uneasiness, a spiritual dissatisfaction, a gnawing awareness that something wasn't quite right. Perhaps I could have blamed the surrounding culture, the pernicious influence of the world, yet that wasn't it. In fact, I sensed the problem most keenly in the last place you'd expect—in church. No church is perfect. Like the saying goes, if you find the perfect church you should leave, because if you stay it won't be perfect anymore. But as I sat in most of these churches, I felt that something was off, and it went beyond personal taste or youthful idealism.

It was my wife who finally put her finger on the problem. "There's no sense of the sacred," she said, "of God's holiness."

## CLOSE ENCOUNTERS

If that sense of divine holiness I longed for seemed absent in my church experiences, it leaped from the pages of Scripture. The Bible is filled with kings and beggars, prophets and prostitutes, warriors and weaklings, merchants and thieves. But when they encountered God, or even one of his angelic envoys, they reacted in remarkably similar ways. They trembled. They cowered. Some went mute. The ones who could manage speech expressed despair (or "woe," to use a biblical word) and were convinced they were about to die.

Fainters abound in Scripture. Take the prophet Daniel, for instance. He could stare down lions, but when the heavens opened before him, he swooned like a Victorian lady. Ezekiel, too, was overwhelmed by his vision of God. After witnessing Yahweh's throne chariot lift into the air with the sound of a jet engine, he fell face-first to the ground. When Solomon dedicated the temple, the glory of the Lord was so overpowering "the priests could not perform their service" (1 Kings 8:11).

New Testament types fared no better. John's revelations on the island of Patmos left him lying on the ground "as though dead" (Rev. 1:17). The disciples dropped when they saw Jesus transfigured. Even the intrepid Saul marching to Damascus collapsed before the blazing brilliance of the resurrected Christ.

How different from our popular depictions. In movies, angels are warm, approachable. Teddy bears with wings. God is Morgan Freeman or some other avuncular presence. Scripture, however, knows nothing of such portrayals. Divine encounters were terrifying, leaving even the most stout and spiritual vibrating with fear—or lying facedown, unconscious.

It may not be pleasant to think about these kinds of encounters. It isn't comforting. You won't find the passages of Scripture previously referenced on plaques that hang in living rooms and church foyers. They're absent from most devotionals and even most sermons. I understand why it's tempting to skip them altogether. Fast-forward to more assuring passages. But that's a mistake. We can't fully appreciate God's grace and love until we consider his holiness, his otherness. Pastor Matt Chandler wrote, "The work of God in the cross of Christ strikes us as awe-inspiring only after we have first been awed by the glory of God."[1]

That's why we need to be jarred by God's glory. Astonished afresh by his majesty. Staggered by his power. If we ever hope to trade the shallows for the deep, we must rediscover the holiness of God.

## HOLY, HOLY, HOLY

One of the most powerful descriptions of God is found in Isaiah 6. In most Bibles the passage is titled "Isaiah's Commission." This is a classic example of burying the lead. Yes, these verses record Isaiah's prophetic calling, but first we see one of the most beautiful and harrowing images of God in all literature. Here it is in Isaiah's words:

> In the year that King Uzziah died, I saw the Lord, high and exalted, seated on a throne; and the train of his robe filled the temple. Above him were seraphim, each with six wings: With two wings they covered their faces, with two they

covered their feet, and with two they were flying. And they were calling to one another:

"Holy, holy, holy is the LORD Almighty;
the whole earth is full of his glory."

At the sound of their voices the doorposts and thresholds shook and the temple was filled with smoke. (vv. 1–4)

The sight of the seraphim alone would make most mortals tremble. This is the only time in Scripture we see these mysterious beings. Their name, *seraphim*, literally means "fiery, burning ones."[2] This may be a reference to their appearance. Perhaps flames leaped from their bodies, or they radiated celestial light. Maybe the name simply points to their function. As we see in subsequent verses, they serve not only as heralds of God's holiness but also as agents of purification.

Then there's their anatomy, peculiar even for celestial creatures. Aren't angels supposed to have only one set of wings? These angels possessed three sets. Apparently the sight of the Lord Almighty enthroned and clothed in divine regalia is too intense even for the hosts of heaven. The seraphim used their extra wings to shield their faces and feet from God as they cried out blindly, "Holy, holy, holy." These were antiphonal cries, an ancient sort of call-and-response likely similar to a practice of the early Hebrews. The repetition of the word *holy* is significant. Some hear an early trinitarian echo. All agree that the triplicate cry gives emphasis. Apparently one *holy* just wouldn't do.

The cries of the seraphim shook the temple. Isaiah shook too.

Woe to me! . . . I am ruined! For I am a man of unclean lips, and I live among a people of unclean lips, and my eyes have seen the King, the LORD Almighty. (v. 5)

What was happening to Isaiah? R. C. Sproul explained: "What Isaiah was expressing is what modern psychologists describe as the experience of personal disintegration."[3] In other words, he was falling apart, having a breakdown, freaking out. Isaiah's reaction may seem odd, but before we label him a coward, consider how German theologian Rudolf Otto described such encounters in his classic, *The Idea of the Holy*. Otto coined a term for what Isaiah experienced—the *mysterium tremendum*, the overwhelming mystery. Or as Otto put it, "the mystery before which men tremble." According to Otto, holiness includes "absolute unapproachability . . . absolute overpoweringness . . . awful majesty."[4]

At this point we might expect the seraphim to swoop down and comfort Isaiah. Maybe even throw an arm around his shoulder and say, "Calm down, Isaiah. What's all this talk about unclean lips? God's cool with you just the way you are."

That's what I would expect to happen. After all, Isaiah was the godliest person in Israel. He was chosen to be the very mouthpiece of the Lord. Why would he be in danger of death because he caught a glimpse of God?

But the angels didn't seem to share my perspective. They did little to assuage Isaiah's fears. In fact, they seemed to acknowledge the gravity of his predicament. It was not safe for him, a sinful mortal, to behold the unmediated glory of God.

Death or cleansing—these were the only two solutions for

Isaiah's predicament. Fortunately for Isaiah, the seraphim chose the latter.

> Then one of the seraphim flew to me with a live coal in his hand, which he had taken with tongs from the altar. With it he touched my mouth and said, "See, this has touched your lips; your guilt is taken away and your sin atoned for." (vv. 6–7)

Finishing this passage feels like waking from a dream . . . or a nightmare. Odd creatures, a trembling temple filled with smoke, and at the center of it all, the Lord Almighty, devastating in his glory. Harder to look at than the sun. What a vision! What a powerful, lofty image of God!

## LOSING ALTITUDE

Shortly after studying this passage, I visited a local bookstore. While perusing titles on the Recent Releases table, one book caught my eye. It was *Help, Thanks, Wow* by best-selling author Anne Lamott. I have enjoyed Lamott's writing in the past, both on Christian spirituality and the craft of writing. But as I started to read her latest work, I was disappointed by what seemed to be a flippant attitude about the nature of God. After meditating on Isaiah's majestic vision, Lamott's words seemed overly casual, maybe even dangerously casual. Early in the book, she acknowledged that some readers balk at the very idea of God. So she endeavored to ease their apprehension.

Nothing could matter less than what we call this force [God]. I know some ironic believers who call God Howard, as in "Our Father, who are in Heaven, Howard be thy name." I called God Phil for a long time, after a Mexican bracelet maker promised to write, "Phil 4:4-7" on my bracelet, Philippians 4:4-7 being my favorite passage of Scripture, but got only as far as "Phil" before having to dismantle his booth. Phil is a great name for God.

My friend Robyn calls God "the Grandmothers." The Deteriorata, a parody of the Desiderata, counsels us, "Therefore, make peace with your god, / Whatever you conceive him to be—/ Hairy thunderer, or cosmic muffin."

Let's not get bogged down on whom or what we pray to. Let's just say prayer is communication from our hearts to the great mystery, or Goodness, or Howard.[5]

I cringed at these words. The god Lamott described is highly malleable, personal or impersonal (take your pick), and when it comes to the name of this god, "nothing could matter less." In the Bible, God is unchanging, highly personal, and when it comes to his identity, nothing could matter more. I appreciate Lamott's encouraging people to pray. Unfortunately, in pursuing that goal, she created a god who isn't worth praying to.

If it sounds like I'm being hard on Lamott, it's because I've glimpsed the same tendency in myself and in those around me. I'm an evangelical, and we pride ourselves on taking the Bible and the God of the Bible seriously. But listen to our worship songs. Many are trite and shallow, with lyrics that could be sung to God or a girlfriend. We write evermore effusive, saccharine lyrics about God's affection. We assure ourselves that even if no one else were on earth, Jesus would have died "just for me," a bizarre, unbiblical speculation. We write books about God's "obsession with you."[6] Our church experiences often reinforce this one-sided, individualistic view of God. Thomas E. Bergler, author of *The Juvenilization of American Christianity*, described a typical evangelical worship service:

> The house lights go down. Spinning, multicolored lights sweep the auditorium. A rock band launches into a rousing opening song. "Ignore everyone else, this time is just about you and Jesus," proclaims the lead singer. The music changes to a slow dance tune, and the people sing about falling in love with Jesus. A guitarist sporting skinny jeans and a soul patch closes the worship set with a prayer, beginning, "Hey God . . ." The spotlight then falls on the speaker, who tells entertaining stories, cracks a few jokes, and assures everyone that "God is not mad at you. He loves you unconditionally."[7]

The language we use reveals an awful lot about how we think about God. A cursory examination of the way we speak exposes how pervasive this Jesus-as-my-nonjudgmental-buddy attitude is in the church. For many of my peers, God is the big guy upstairs. Jesus is our homeboy. I talked to one recent graduate of a Christian college who referred to Jesus repeatedly as "the J man." I've heard young women declare they are remaining single for a season because they are "dating Jesus." I didn't have the heart to point out that to date Jesus would mean he would have to first divorce the church.

Pastor Lillian Daniel wrote a cutting parody exposing our

casual view of Jesus. Here is a description of one Sunday featured in her "Church Calendar: New and Improved."

> *Jesus, My Buddy! Sunday, November 20 (formerly Christ the King Sunday)*: Images will be chosen to emphasize the ordinariness of Jesus and to boost church members' self-esteem. By way of pastoral care, members will be given the opportunity to come forward to share and to unpack their lingering feelings of inadequacy resulting from previous presentations of a transcendent ruler God. This service should offer the comforting message that God is really no better than we are.[8]

Like I said, this is satire. Thankfully, as of yet there is no Jesus, My Buddy! Sunday. But the parody works precisely because it underscores a serious point—we tend to embrace the idea of a divine friend but become squeamish about the notion of a transcendent God.

The 2008 novel *The Shack* took the Christian world by storm, selling more than 15 million copies. It portrayed God the Father as "Papa," a "large, beaming, African-American woman," a veritable clone of the sassy but soothing Tess from the TV show *Touched by an Angel*. Much of the novel recounted conversations the main character, Mack, had with Papa as she bustled about the kitchen, preparing food. Papa warned Mack that consuming too many greens would "give him the trots." When Jesus dropped a bowl of pancake batter and splattered Papa's skirt, she playfully chided "greasy fingers" for his clumsiness.[9] Whatever your view of the book's theology, it would be hard to argue it does justice to the holiness and otherness of God.

I'm sorry if I sound like a curmudgeon. I don't mean to. The expressions cited above may not be wrong in and of themselves. But I find they are rarely balanced by a sense of reverence and awe. There's nothing wrong with applying intimate language to our relationship with Jesus. The disciple John described himself as "the disciple whom Jesus loved" and was depicted as laying his head on Jesus' chest (John 13:23). Yet when that same disciple beheld the resurrected Christ in a vision on the island of Patmos, he "fell at his feet as though dead" (Rev. 1:17). We need intimacy with Christ—and reverence for him. But I fear we've lost the second half of that equation.

Recently I was in a worship service where the pastor invited congregants to call out God's attributes. He asked us to finish this sentence: "Lord, you are . . ."

The responses came in rapid succession: "Loving!" said someone. "Merciful," added another. "Gracious." . . . "Kind." . . . "Compassionate." . . .

All true. Yet what I found interesting was what *wasn't* said. There wasn't a word about God's holiness, not a whisper about his justice, let alone his wrath. Had Isaiah been in attendance, perhaps he would have added, "Terrifying."

## GOD STRANGE AGAIN

There are no experts on God.

Not me. Not you. Not your pastor or the theology professor with two PhDs.

*Merriam-Webster* defines an *expert* as "one with the special skill or knowledge representing mastery of a particular subject."[10]

Have you ever met someone who possesses "mastery" on the topic of God?

Me neither.

While we know enough about God to receive salvation and enter into a relationship with him, our knowledge of him is still far from complete. Our intelligence is too small, our languages too limited. When it comes to God, we're all beginners. Yet this very realization—that we cannot fully understand God—is crucial to even beginning to understand him.

The early church father Gregory of Nyssa compared contemplating God's nature to standing at the edge of a sheer cliff with no foothold. He wrote:

> The soul . . . becomes dizzy and perplexed and returns once again to what is natural to it, content now to merely know this about the Transcendent, that it is completely different from the nature of the things which the soul knows.[11]

We might assume knowing God simply includes getting all our facts about him straight. But maybe the first step is vertigo, a holy disorientation. Perhaps only once we've been shocked out of our normal way of processing reality—categorizing it, mastering it—can we hope to gain even a glimpse of God's awesome power and beauty. Even C. S. Lewis, arguably the most brilliant Christian of the last century, speculated that "half our great theological and metaphysical problems" would be too confused to even have answers. "How many hours are in a mile? Is yellow square or round? Probably half the questions we ask . . . are like that."[12]

Our attempts to describe God stretch the limits of human

language. The best descriptions seem to veer toward the superlative and abstract. Theologians describe God as the ground of all being, the uncaused first cause, the overwhelming mystery. How could we possibly hope to comprehend such a Being? Our brains are too puny, our resources too limited. The moment we think we have God figured out is the instant of our greatest confusion. As the Dominican priest Victor White wrote:

> So soon as we become satisfied with any picture of God, we are in danger of idolatry: of mistaking the comprehensible image for the reality, of losing the numinous, the mystery, the transcendent majesty of God. So soon as, consciously or unconsciously, we suppose we have grasped God, he must elude us, for he is always beyond the furthermost advance we make in knowledge about him.[13]

Don't get me wrong. We can feel God's presence and receive his love. We can know him, but that's only possible because, in a stunning display of mercy, he chose to reveal himself to us in ways we could understand. However, possessing this modicum of knowledge should never be confused with comprehensive understanding. Ultimately, when it comes to God, we're like ants crawling across an iPad: in touch with something we only faintly understand.

Literary critic Jonathan Culler defined poetry as "the making strange of language." What does he mean by "making strange"? Simply that, in poems, words draw attention to themselves. With other kinds of reading (an instruction manual, for instance) words serve merely to convey information. But in poetry, words become the stars. They don't disappear behind their meanings.

Instead, through literary devices such as meter, rhyme, repetition, and structure, poetry "foregrounds language itself: makes it strange, thrusts it at you—Look! I'm language!"[14]

The Bible does the same thing for God. It thrusts God at you, saying, "Look! This is God!" It makes God strange. Not strange in a bad way but in the most basic sense of the word— unfamiliar, other, outside the range of our knowing.

Unfortunately, in our efforts to make the Bible interesting and relevant, we try to normalize God. We become experts at taking something lofty, so unfathomable and incomprehensible, and dragging it down to the lowest shelf. We fail to account for the fact that God is neither completely knowable nor remotely manageable.

This habit is not confined to the pews. Those of us who lead can be the worst. Preaching professor John Koessler wrote of the tendency for preachers to "normalize the outrageous in Scripture."[15] There's a temptation to flatten out the divine portrayals in the Bible to make God more palatable to our audiences. We're in desperate need of leaders who will resist this temptation and teach the "whole counsel of God" (Acts 20:27 ESV), holiness included.

Here's the beautiful irony: making God strange actually enables us to know him more. Once we have marveled at his magnitude and mystery, we are able to achieve the deep intimacy that grows out of a true appreciation for who God is. Instead of treating him as an equal, we approach him with reverent awe. Only when we've been awestruck by his majesty can we be overwhelmed by his love.

# FOUR
# A VISION OF HOLINESS

**ONE OF AMERICA'S MOST PRIZED ARTISTIC TREASURES WAS** created by a janitor.

The elaborate arrangement is housed at the Smithsonian American Art Museum in Washington, DC. Its creator was James Hampton, an African-American bachelor who was virtually unknown during his life.

The piece, called *The Throne of the Third Heaven*, has been called "America's greatest work of visionary art."[1] Yet it's made entirely of junk.

*The Throne* is a recreation of God's throne room described in the book of Revelation. It was discovered only after Hampton's death in 1964. Reminiscent of a cathedral chancel, the arrangement has 180 pieces, including a throne, altar, offertory tables, pulpits, mercy seats, and other sacred objects. The work appears to sparkle with gold and silver. In reality it consists entirely of discarded items: old furniture, cigarette boxes, wine bottles, used light bulbs, scraps of insulation board, jelly glasses, hollow cardboard cylinders, construction paper, and desk blotters—all tacked together with glue, tape, and pins, then covered with gold and aluminum foil. Over the course of fourteen years, Hampton collected the materials from secondhand stores or fished them from trash cans.

Little is known about Hampton or his motives for creating *The Throne*. He mentioned the project only in passing to friends and coworkers. Yet the inscription found on the wall of the rented garage where he assembled the work provides a clue. The words are taken from Proverbs 29:18: "Where there is no vision, the people perish" (KJV).

Hampton's masterpiece is stunning. But the story behind it is even more remarkable. Hampton, a devout man who harbored dreams of becoming a minister, wanted to give people a vision of God's grandeur. And he felt it was so important that every day after a long shift of mopping floors and cleaning toilets, he toiled to transform a dingy garage into a holy vision.

Hampton was onto something. We need a vision of God. Not one suspended in the heavens, but one that stays with us in our daily lives.

So far we've considered some stunning images of God. We've trembled with the Israelites as God descended in fire on Mount Sinai. We've peered over Isaiah's shoulder to catch a glimpse of the Lord enthroned and exalted. We've briefly considered what these appearances mean about God and his character. Now let's explore what it all means for us. It's one thing to marvel at God's holiness from afar. But what difference does a holy God make on the ground?

## REDEEMING HOLINESS

Unfortunately, in contemporary times, the word *holiness* has gotten a bad reputation. For many, the word connotes spiritual superiority. It's pejorative, a term used to describe someone with a holier than thou, judgmental attitude. Or they may think holy roller, another derogatory label applied to hyper-religious people prone to venting spiritual excitement with sudden outbursts and violent body movements.

Given these bizarre and misguided associations, it's essential to clear the fog surrounding this ancient word.

In the Bible *holiness* has two primary meanings. One meaning is moral perfection, what Scripture calls "righteousness." For instance, the writer of Hebrews told us that while Jesus was on earth, he was "tempted in every way, just as we are—yet he did not sin" (4:15). In other words, Jesus lived a sinless or completely *holy* life.

We see this dimension of holiness in Isaiah 6. After his vision of God, Isaiah realizes he has a problem. There's a dangerous discontinuity between himself and God. It's not merely about God's power and grandeur. Isaiah is concerned with the ethical divide. He fears he's doomed because he has "unclean lips" (v. 5). It seems that a revelation of God is accompanied by an overpowering sense of God's purity—and a corresponding awareness of our own sinfulness. The preceding chapter also reveals this ethical element of holiness. "But the Lord Almighty will be exalted by his justice, / and the holy God will be proved holy by his righteous acts" (Isa. 5:16). Moral perfection is a crucial component of God's holiness.

While this element of holiness is clear in the Bible, it has

43

become murky in the church. Pastor Kevin DeYoung argues that we have a "hole in our holiness." He's not just talking about immorality per se; he sees our lack of concern about holiness as the problem. "The hole in our holiness," he explains, "is that we don't really care about it."[2]

One nationwide study found that "the concept of holiness baffles most Americans." When asked to describe what it means to be holy, the most common reply was "I don't know." Of those identified by the study as "born again," only 46 percent believed "God has called them to holiness." The study's conclusion was candid: "The results portray a body of Christians who attend church and read the Bible, but do not understand the concept or significance of holiness, do not personally desire to be holy, and therefore do little, if anything to pursue it."[3]

I find it telling that *strive* has become a dirty word in Christian circles, even though Scripture repeatedly commands us to strive for godliness (Acts 24:16; 1 Thess. 5:15). The Greek word translated "strive" is *agonizomai*, and it implies an agonizing, intense, purposeful struggle.[4] Each time it appears in the New Testament, it's used in a positive way, as a means to attaining true holiness. If we care about personal holiness at all, we tend to assume it demands passivity. We think that God will sanctify us unilaterally, without asking us to lift a finger.

Younger Christians in particular seem to view the pursuit of holiness as optional or even legalistic. Twentysomething Christian writer Tyler Braun had this to say about his generation:

As the next generation of young Christians (including myself) continues to root themselves well within culture, we've lost the marks that allow Christ to be seen by a world that denies Him. We've lost holiness. Young believers have pursued life experience at the expense of innocence as we've given up on caring about the sin in our own lives.[5]

Young-culture critic Brett McCracken worries too. He sees young evangelicals compensating for the fundamentalism of yesteryear by acting no differently than their unbelieving counterparts.

> When I go to parties with Christian friends, and then parties with non-Christian friends, I often lament that they are observably indistinguishable. We are the same in how we talk: the petty subjects of conversation, the toxic cynicism lacing our speech, the obscene language, the general negativity . . . same.[6]

His diagnosis and suggested cure are well worth reading.

Why is there such a lack of discernible holiness? Why this confusion on a basic Christian teaching? For Braun, the problem traces back to a lopsided understanding of God. "We picture God only as a God who provides mercy, not judgment. So of course we can get away with our sin, because God forgives."[7]

I believe he's right. And not just about the younger generation. This thinking pervades the church. Why? We lack a practice of personal holiness because we've lost a theology of divine holiness. When we neglect a part of God's nature, we shouldn't be surprised when that same attribute goes missing in our lives. Missionary Lesslie Newbigin saw a clear link between God's holiness and ours:

We need to see this God of Israel both in his wrath and his infinite mercy. We need to learn a holiness that rejects all compromise with evil and a generosity that seeks and saves the lost. We need to learn to know God as he is.[8]

The Bible repeatedly makes explicit the connection between God's holiness and ours. "Be holy," God says, "because I . . . am holy" (Lev. 19:2). The New Testament echoes this theme. "Just as he who called you is holy, so be holy in all you do" (1 Pet. 1:15).

We will never be perfect. Not on this side of eternity. But when we gain a fuller vision of God, our lives will begin to reflect his holiness. As Braun concluded, "We are holy because of His holiness being worked out within us."[9]

## THE REFLEX OF WORSHIP

Have you ever sensed God in a room?

I think I have. Sounds strange, I know. But if you've participated in enough corporate worship or prayer, you may know what I mean. And hopefully you'll sympathize with how difficult it is to explain.

The first word that comes to mind is *lightness*. There's a certain levity that pervades the room, this sense that you could almost climb into the air. At the same time (and here's where things get odd), there's a heaviness. Not a bad heaviness, like gloom. It's a good heaviness. The air feels heavy—thick with God, if you'll forgive the expression. Perhaps it's no coincidence that the Hebrew word for glory, *kābôd*, comes from a root signifying "weight."[10]

I know such a description will sound hopelessly subjective to an outsider. I wouldn't submit it for proof of God's existence to my skeptical friends. Yet if you've experienced it, there's no denying God's presence. It's palpable, vivid. As clear as the nose on your face.

God is always present, I believe. But he doesn't always manifest his presence in quite the same way. The remarkable thing about these experiences is that they seem to take me by surprise. In those services in which I have sensed his presence, it wasn't because the music was particularly good or the prayers especially profound. It was because there was a collective sense of God's power and glory, of his holiness. I recall standing in a room with three hundred people singing "How Great Is Our God" and feeling like we were blending into heaven. Only an intense appreciation for God's holiness produces such moments.

We go to great lengths to create atmospheres conducive to meaningful worship. Each year we publish hundreds of new books on worship, hold conferences, and spend millions of dollars on instruments and décor we hope will lead people into the presence of God. None of this is wrong. Atmosphere is important. But I believe that no matter how much we invest, from stained glass to strobe lights, without an appreciation of God's holiness, our worship is fated to be superficial and, at best, momentarily moving.

"Ultimately transcendence is what makes a worship service meaningful," wrote pastor and author Bill Giovannetti.[11] He's absolutely right. When we glimpse God's holiness, it produces wonder. We begin approaching God with "reverence and awe" because we see him as "a consuming fire" (Heb. 12:28–29).

Worship is the natural reflex of mortals to the presence of a holy God. When God shows up, worship doesn't have to be manufactured or drummed up. It happens instinctively. And it's rich and authentic. As worship leader Matt Redman put it, "Worship thrives on wonder. For worship to be worship, it must contain something of the otherness of God."[12] A vision of God's holiness is essential to our worship. It rescues our worship from superficiality and makes it passionate and profound. If we had a vision of God like Isaiah did, I don't think we'd be asking him for good parking spots.

Of course this principle is not confined to what happens during the worship set on Sunday mornings. God's holiness provides the fuel for our entire spiritual journeys. A friend of mine shared how an understanding of God's holiness impacted her. "I had accepted Christ as a teenager," she said, "but it was a sort of casual thing, like 'Okay, I believe.'" Then her relationship with Christ deepened when she read A. W. Tozer's spiritual classic, *The Knowledge of the Holy*. "I had started a relationship with God. But until I read that book, I didn't really understand who God was. After understanding a little about God's holiness, things changed. Suddenly I began to understand who I had a relationship with."

"Where there is no vision, the people perish." Like the janitor-artist Hampton, most people quote the King James Version of Proverbs 29:18. As much as I love the poetic cadences of the King James, this is one instance where the famous translation misses the mark. The context and content of the verse make it clear this isn't just any "vision" the people need. A better translation would read: "Without a vision *of God*, the people perish." It's God himself who makes worship meaningful. It's a vision of his holiness that drives us to our knees. God's holiness is the heart of our worship.

Earlier I mentioned that theologian Rudolf Otto described the experience of the holy as the *mysterium tremendum*. That is the phrase that became popular, but his original description was longer. He called it the *mysterium tremendum et fascinates*—"the overwhelming mystery that fascinates or attracts." These Latin words capture a paradoxical truth about God's holiness. It overwhelms, but it also draws. It terrifies and captivates. It bows our heads even as it lifts our hearts. Ultimately, it results in joyful and reverent worship.

## RIGHTEOUSNESS RELIEF

When I was in high school, I tried to convert my friend to Christianity. It wasn't going well. I wasn't much of an evangelist, and he was a hard case. When he told me he didn't believe in God, I could only think of one biblical rejoinder: "The fool says in his heart / 'There is no God'" (Ps. 14:1). Since my friend outweighed me by about twenty pounds and liked to fight, I decided to keep the verse to myself.

Nothing seemed to get through to him. Nothing except this: I described to him, as best I could, the experience of forgiveness. "There's nothing like coming to God with all the bad things you've done and asking for him to cleanse you," I told him. "It's like taking a shower after being dirty for a long time. You feel completely new, totally clean."

He was silent.

"Hey, man. I don't mean to preach at you," I said.

"That doesn't sound like preaching," he replied looking off at something. "It doesn't sound like preaching at all."

Like I said, I wasn't much of an evangelist, but I got one thing right. There's something powerful about the prospect of forgiveness, of being made clean. It's a relief.

John Eldredge acknowledged that relief isn't the first thing that comes to mind when people hear the word *holiness*. As he pointed out, holiness is more often associated with austerity, suffering, and self-denial. So why call it a "relief"? He explained:

> Look at it this way: Ask the anorexic young girl how she would feel if she simply no longer struggled with food, diet, exercise—if she simply never even gave it another thought. Ask the man consumed with jealousy how he would feel if he woke one day to discover that all he once felt jealous over was simply gone. Ask the raging person what it would be like to be free of rage or the alcoholic what it would be like to be completely free from addiction. Take the things you struggle with and ask yourself, 'What would life be like if I never even struggled with this again?' It would be an utter relief. An absolute utter relief.[13]

Throughout history people have suffered mightily in pursuit of holiness. They've given up fortunes, fought battles, embarked on grueling pilgrimages, and whipped themselves bloody. Maybe that's why we see holiness as something threatening and burdensome. Something reserved for those with iron wills and saintly bearings. Yes, holiness requires effort, but we tend to forget what Eldredge observed: that holiness is actually an utter relief. An absolute utter relief.

## IDENTITY ISSUES

A second way *holiness* is used is to designate someone or something as set apart or "sanctified" for divine service.[14] In fact, the Hebrew word for holiness, *qodêsh*, is derived from the root *qad*, which means "to cut" or "to be separated".[15] This is the far more common meaning of holiness in Scripture. We hear it in the song of Moses:

> *Who among the gods*
> *is like you, LORD?*
> *Who is like you—*
> *majestic in holiness,*
> *awesome in glory,*
> *working wonders? (Ex. 15:11)*

And again, in Hannah's prayer:

> *There is no one holy like the LORD;*
> *there is no one besides you;*
> *there is no Rock like our God. (1 Sam. 2:2)*

The authors of Scripture visit this theme repeatedly. And God himself stresses his distinct status. "I am the LORD; that is my name! / I will not yield my glory to another / or my praise to idols" (Isa. 42:8).

Bible scholar Louis Berkhof explained, "The holiness of God is first of all that divine perfection by which He is absolutely distinct from all His creatures, and is exalted above them in infinite majesty."[16]

We also see this focus—being set apart—in Isaiah's vision. Here God was separated, literally. Isaiah saw the Lord "high and exalted" (6:1), probably in the sky, above the temple. And just in case this stunning display failed to communicate God's eminence, he was adorned in kingly attire with a train that flowed from his throne, filling the temple.

As we've discussed, this vision gives us insight into the nature of God. It also helps us understand our identity. Holiness entails set-apartness, otherness. Otherness is a concept that is used by social scientists to understand the identities of individuals or whole groups of people. Here's the idea: we do not exist in a vacuum. Rather, our identities emerge as we define ourselves in contrast to others. The ultimate "Other" is God. As Christians, it's imperative that we orient ourselves in light of his nature.

Of course viewing ourselves in reference to God can be depressing. We look at God's holiness and despair. Compared to God, we are nothing—sinful and powerless, certainly not the divine beings of New Age fancy. Yet this realization is important to guard against delusions. It helps us resist that ancient human tendency to pull God down to our level. Theologian Marva J. Dawn explained why this tendency is so engrained in the Western world:

> As our culture has worked hard to establish equality among persons, we've somehow put God into that parity and gradually reduced our sense that this is a breathtakingly transcendent *GOD* we're talking about.[17]

We need our breath stolen by a glimpse of God's majesty. Only then will we see him Isaiah did, as "the High and Lofty

One who inhabits eternity" (57:15 NKJV), rather than fashioning idols that bear our likeness. A proper knowledge of God's holiness is essential for knowing him as he really is, and who we really are.

On the other hand, since this great God loves us, we have inestimable worth. We are made in his image, and, as the psalmist exuded, "crowned . . . with glory and honor" (Ps. 8:5). These twin truths humble us and lift our heads, guarding against both pride and insecurity. They remind us that though we are merely children, our Father is the King.

## RELIEF AND JOY

It's important to note how Isaiah responded to his vision of God. At first he was overwhelmed and cried out, "Woe to me! I am ruined" (6:5). But the passage didn't end in despair. After the majestic appearance, the Lord spoke:

"Whom shall I send? And who will go for us?" (v. 8).

At this point Isaiah moved beyond fear. Dismay became determination. After beholding the glory of God, Isaiah did not need a pep rally or motivational speech. He was eager to accept the mission God had for him.

"Here am I. Send me!" he says (v. 8). The vision of God resulted in a willingness, even eagerness, to serve God.

I was watching a TV show recently in which one of the characters was struggling with whether to go through with an arranged marriage. In his home country arranged marriages were the norm. But after living in America, he was having second thoughts about adhering to this ancient custom, especially since he'd never met his wife-to-be. Still, when she flew into the airport, he dutifully waited for her, flowers in hand, and a gloomy expression on his face. But when she stepped through the terminal, everything changed. She was beautiful! Suddenly his glum demeanor disappeared. The thought of marrying this woman was no longer a dreaded duty; it was a delight. What had changed? He'd seen her.

Often we serve God out of obligation. We drag ourselves to church, force ourselves to serve others—but our hearts aren't in it. We're like that guy at the airport, grudgingly holding flowers for God. We're trying to live holy lives because we know we should, but it's burdensome, joyless.

What can change this? Seeing God. When we get a vision of who God truly is, suddenly we're energized to do his mission. Once we gaze upon his grandeur and glory, obedience becomes easy. It's not a duty—it's a joy. We want to live for him. Our voices join Isaiah's willing reply, "Here I am! Send me."

# FIVE
# DANGEROUS LIVING

**DANIEL WALKER VISITS BROTHELS. BUT NOT FOR THE REASON** you think.

After serving as a detective in New Zealand for twenty years, Walker now uses his law enforcement skills to tackle the evils of sex trafficking. When I spoke with him, Walker had spent four years traveling the globe infiltrating brothels to gather evidence and put away traffickers.

His strategy was simple. He would identify brothels he suspected of trafficking and enter them posing as a customer. Wearing a hidden camera, he would pay for a girl and submit a recording of the transaction to local authorities. The evidence he collected, along with his personal testimony, freed hundreds of women and girls and led to the prosecution of many of their captors.

As you might imagine, it was dangerous work, physically and spiritually. He had to travel to rough neighborhoods and navigate the seedy underworld of the sex industry. Thugs and pimps were constantly suspicious of this man—unlike the rest of their clientele—who paid for girls only to have conversations with them. There were many close calls. He told me about how during one of his early missions to a brothel in the most dangerous part of Tolima, Colombia, he found himself paralyzed with fear.

"I didn't know what would happen in this brothel as a good Christian boy from New Zealand," he admitted to me. "I was afraid of the bad guys with guns—and there were bad guys with guns—and I was afraid of evil. This was a place where the demonic reigned."

To keep his cover intact, Walker danced with a girl he guessed was no more than sixteen. As he danced, he prayed silently. Then he had an epiphany that dispelled his fear. He told me, "The tables turned when suddenly I saw this prostitute not as a threat to my purity or professionalism, but as a child of God whom he greatly loved. I was filled with this all-consuming, holy hatred for the way evil had ensnared her small life, a holy anger in a world that allows its children to be sold as playthings for the lusts of men. I captured on my covert camera enough evidence to put the bad guys in jail. If anyone was dangerous in that place, it was me."

As he told me the story, a smile crept across his face.

"How much different would it be if Christians saw themselves as the dangerous ones?" he said. "We are bearers of the most wild, dangerous, untamed force for good in the world!"

## INCONVENIENT TRUTH

I attended a public university where the intellectual climate was decidedly secular. Even students who believed in a God seemed to find the idea of a holy God who judges sin absurd. "Sure, I believe there's a God up there," a fellow student told me, "but not the kind who judges people or cares about what I do."

We are reluctant to acknowledge, let alone celebrate, a dangerous God.

I get that. When words like *danger* get too close to *God*, we get nervous. It's not difficult to see why. We live in a time of religious terrorism, clergy abuse scandals, and crooked televangelists. Religious authority has two black eyes and a broken nose. In this environment, talk of God's dangerous qualities tramples all kinds of cultural taboos.

Even committed Christians struggle with God's difficult attributes. When the committee tasked with developing a new hymnal for the Presbyterian Church (USA) met, a debate erupted over whether to include the popular, modern hymn, "In Christ Alone." One line from the song gave the committee pause: "Till on that cross as Jesus died / the wrath of God was satisfied." The committee considered adopting an alternative version designed to eliminate the song's mention of divine wrath: "as Jesus died / the love of God was magnified." But the song's authors would not approve the alteration. In the end, the committee voted to exclude the song from the new hymnals.[1]

Pastors, too, awkwardly negotiate biblical passages that portray divine wrath or choose to avoid them altogether, opting to focus exclusively on grace and love. Some feel obliged to apologize for God. I sympathize with waffling preachers. To modern ears, parts of the Old Testament in particular sound foreign and offensive. In the prophetic books, God rages against Israel's unfaithfulness. The Psalms teem with imprecatory prayers, raw cries for God to rain down vengeance on the wicked.

Fleeing the Old Testament is of little use. The New Testament offers ample evidence of a dangerous God as well. The Gospels record Jesus prophesying doom for unrepentant cities. In the book of Acts the Holy Spirit strikes Ananias and Sapphira dead in a seemingly capricious act of judgment. In Revelation Christ appears with eyes "like blazing fire" (19:12) and a double-edged sword protruding from his mouth. In the later chapters of the book, God's wrath rises to an apocalyptic boil, spilling out on the earth.

If we are honest, many of us don't take these aspects of God as seriously as we should. This is one area where we prefer the safe lagoon to the deep waters.

## FEAR AND FOLLOWING

Croatian theologian Miroslav Volf used to reject the concept of God's wrath. To him, the idea of an angry God was barbaric and backward. But Volf changed his mind when his country experienced a brutal war. As he reflected on the atrocities committed by his countrymen, he came to see God's wrath not just as acceptable but also as necessary:

> My last resistance to the idea of God's wrath was a casualty
> of the war in the former Yugoslavia, the region from which

I come. According to some estimates, 200,000 people were killed and over 3,000,000 were displaced. My villages and cities were destroyed, my people shelled day in and day out, some of them brutalized beyond imagination, and I could not imagine God not being angry.

Though I used to complain about the indecency of the idea of God's wrath, I came to think that I would have to rebel against a God who wasn't wrathful at the sight of the world's evil. God isn't wrathful in spite of being love. God is wrathful because God is love.[2]

As Volf came to realize, only a God who punishes evil and rights wrongs is ultimately a God of love.

It's not just the wicked who have to think about a dangerous God. The Bible repeatedly commands "the fear of the Lord" for anyone who hopes to know him. This fear is not something to overcome or counsel away. It is something to be sought. Scripture maintains that the fear of the Lord brings wisdom, long life, righteousness, and other blessings.[3] This isn't merely a shaking-in-your-boots kind of fear, though we certainly see examples of that in Scripture. Rather "the fear of the Lord" suggests a sense of sobriety toward God, a down-in-your-gut reverence. To fear the Lord is to be grounded in reality, to have an accurate view of God's holy nature and his awesome power.

John Piper used an analogy to explain the fear of the Lord. Imagine hiking across a glacier, he wrote, when a brutal storm whips up. Terrified, you seek shelter and find a cleft in the ice where you can ride out the storm in safety. From that sheltered position, Piper invited readers to imagine how they might feel about the storm:

> Even though [you are] secure, the awesome might of the storm
> rages on, and you watch it with a kind of trembling pleasure as
> it surges out across the distant glaciers. Not everything we call
> fear vanishes from your heart, only the life-threatening part.
> There remains the trembling, the awe, the wonder, the feeling
> that you would never want to tangle with such a storm or be
> the adversary of such a power.[4]

I like that picture. It captures something of the healthy respect we should have for God. To fear the Lord is not to suggest God is callous or cruel. Just the opposite, in fact. It is God's consuming love that makes him so dangerous. Because he cares deeply for his creation, he will not tolerate evil and injustice forever. Sin corrupts and destroys what he has created. So when he sees that happening, he is incensed and becomes very dangerous indeed. Like Volf, I find this truth comforting. What kind of God would look indifferently on Auschwitz? Or remain unmoved by child abuse? Or, as Volf wondered, be apathetic about the loss of life in a brutal civil war? Not the God of the Bible. Not the God revealed in Jesus. God's response to evil is always holy anger.

As unpopular or uncomfortable as it might be to speak of a dangerous God, it is crucial we do so. Not only because we need an accurate view of God. And not merely because we wish to reap the incredible rewards promised to those who fear the Lord. Seeing God as dangerous is essential to how we live. As children of our Father in heaven, we, too, are called to be dangerous. I'm not talking about being violent or destructive. But like God, we should be dangerous to evil and injustice, a holy threat to anything that preys on the innocent, crushes the powerless, and enslaves people to sin.

## THE DANGER OF SAFETY

As Daniel Walker told me his story, I felt energized. *That's what the Christian life is about,* I thought. *It's not about insulating yourself in a religious bubble to avoid being tarnished by the world. It's not about hiding from evil. It means working against injustice, confident that light is more powerful than darkness.*

At the same time, I felt a twinge of sadness. Why wasn't I living that kind of dangerous life? I realize not everyone is called to infiltrate brothels. But why did I, and so many of my Christian friends, seem stuck playing spiritual defense? What prevents us from becoming a threat to the kingdom of darkness? Why are so few North American Christians truly dangerous?

Well, for one, I think we are too concerned with our own safety. We are obsessed with it and spare no expense pursuing it. We drive crash-tested cars with side-impact air bags. We vaccinate ourselves against diseases and stock our cabinets with hand sanitizer and medications. We insure our lives, our health, our homes, our cars, our possessions, and even our pets. We purify water that is already safe to drink. We download software to protect our computers and back up our files. We buy security systems for our houses and automobiles. And those are just some of our individual efforts. Every year the United States government spends more than forty-three billion dollars on domestic security, not including military spending.[5]

We Christians are not immune to this safety obsession. I shake my head when I hear the local Christian radio station promise "safe, easy listening with no offensive lyrics." Safe? Our Founder was murdered. No offensive lyrics? Every time Jesus spoke in public, he seemed to incite rage.

Perhaps our preoccupation with safety is seen most clearly by looking at our prayers. I've been in the church all my life. After attending hundreds of church services, prayer meetings, and small group gatherings, I'd have to say that the most popular prayer is the prayer for safety.

I find it interesting that the Gospels record not one instance of Jesus or the disciples praying for physical safety. Yes, Jesus prayed that the disciples would be kept safe "from the evil one" (John 17:15). But given that Jesus also warned his followers that they would be hated, arrested, beaten, and even murdered, I'm guessing the safety he prayed for was of the spiritual, not physical, variety. So while the Gospels barely mention safety, we can't shut up about it. In fact, for some of us, it's the only kind of prayer we utter—that and the one for a better parking spot.

Don't get me wrong. Guarding you and your loved ones against harm is wise. Asking God for protection is too. But when a desire for safety paralyzes us with fear and prevents us from carrying out God's mission, something is wrong. When petitions for safety dominate our prayer lives, it's a sign our spiritual house is not in order.

The early Christians were forced to their knees when threatened, but their prayers were strikingly different. In Acts 4 Peter and John were arrested for preaching Jesus' resurrection from the dead. They were released but threatened and ordered "not to speak or teach at all in the name of Jesus" (v. 18).

These were no idle threats. They knew that to disobey these orders would likely mean further imprisonment, whippings, even death. Peter and John were understandably shaken by the ordeal; when they joined the other believers, they lifted their voices together in fervent prayer. But they didn't pray for safety.

They prayed for boldness. "Now, Lord, consider their threats and enable your servants to speak your word with great boldness" (v. 29). Think about how strange this prayer is for a moment. In response to being threatened, they prayed for the courage to keep doing the very thing that got them in trouble in the first place. Probably not the response I would have.

Such stories are not confined to biblical times. The same kind of commitment is alive and well among our brothers and sisters who live in places where the Christian faith is illegal.

I recently stumbled across an interesting set of questions used by Asian Access, a Christian missions agency in South Asia. Church leaders in the organization use the following questions to determine a new convert's readiness to follow Christ. In the West, we might ask newcomers if they prefer contemporary or traditional worship. As you can see, the questions they ask in other parts of the world are quite different.

- Are you willing to leave home and lose the blessing of your father?
- Are you willing to lose your job?
- Are you willing to go to the village and those who persecute you, forgive them, and share the love of Christ with them?
- Are you willing to give an offering to the Lord?
- Are you willing to be beaten rather than deny your faith?
- Are you willing to go to prison?
- Are you willing to die for Jesus?[6]

Besides making me feel very grateful for where I live (and slightly guilty for feeling grateful), the questions sounded familiar.

I heard an echo of Jesus' words from Luke 14. You know the passage. Jesus spun around to the people following him and asked, "Are you sure you want to do this?"

That's my paraphrase, of course. What Jesus actually said was much worse. If you want to be my disciple, you have to hate your family, take up your cross, count the cost, give up everything—the kind of demands as unwelcome in our day as they were in his.

## VILLAGE GODS

Years ago I volunteered at an event put on by a national youth ministry. The evening was fun but grueling. We bobbed for apples, captured flags, and raced eggs across the floor using only our noses. The games culminated with a frigid indignity: I lay on my back and let three giggling teenagers make an ice cream sundae on my face.

As I toweled chocolate syrup from my chin, a leader ordered the teens into a semicircle. It was time for the devotional, which included a gospel presentation—but it was a gospel presentation that made me want to stand up and scream. "Being a Christian isn't hard," he told the group. "You won't lose your friends or be unpopular at school. Nothing will change. Your life will be the same, just better."

I glanced at the teens. One was flicking Doritos at a friend. Others whispered to one another or stared at the floor. None of them seemed to be listening. *And why should they?* I wondered. Who cares about something that involves no adventure, no sacrifice, and no risk? The leader was selling them a small god, one who demanded nothing of them—and they weren't buying it.

The famous English pastor John Stott told of visiting a rural church in England while on a study leave. He worshipped with them each Sunday and shared in their fellowship. Week after week he heard the pastor address issues facing the village and listened to their prayers concerning their church. They didn't pray for anything beyond the safety of members on vacation and for those recovering from illness. At the end of his visit John Stott came to a sad conclusion. "They were a village people," he said, "and they worshiped a village god."[7]

I'm afraid that's all too common in the church today. We have big buildings, big budgets—and a small god. A village god.

If there was anyone who did not worship a village god, it was the mid-twentieth-century missionary Jim Elliot, who was killed bringing the gospel to the Waodani people of Ecuador. When Elliot observed the safe faith practiced by most Christians of his time, he wrote these words:

> We are so utterly ordinary, so commonplace, while we profess to know a Power the twentieth century does not reckon with. But we are "harmless," and therefore unharmed. We are spiritual pacifists, non-militants, conscientious objectors in this battle-to-the-death with principalities and powers in high places. Meekness must be had for contact with men, but brass, outspoken boldness is required to take part in the comradeship of the Cross. We are "sideliners"—coaching and criticizing the real wrestlers while content to sit by and leave the enemies of God unchallenged. The world cannot hate us, we are too much like its own. Oh that God would make us dangerous![8]

"That God would make us dangerous." That's a good prayer. When safety becomes our driving concern, not only do we fail to live dangerously but our witness to the wider world suffers. We become known solely for what we are against, not what we are for. People identify us by what we won't do, rather than what we will. Sometimes our refusals to do certain things should attract attention. But how much better would it be if we were known by the strange things we are willing to do? Things like loving the unlovely, standing up for the oppressed, returning good for evil or, like the disciples, sharing the good news of Jesus in the teeth of opposition.

It's easy to imagine holiness as a stoic staving off of temptation, a perpetual washing of the hands to keep from being defiled from the world. But holiness is so much more than that. It's full engagement with humanity. It means getting dirty up to your armpits. Holiness is about what you're willing to risk to love others and to see God glorified.

## RISKY BEHAVIOR

One of history's riddles is the explosive growth of the early church. Scholars still puzzle over how an obscure Jewish sect grew to comprise more than half the Roman Empire within a relatively short time.[9] Part of the answer lies in the fact that while fearlessly sharing the gospel, even under persecution, the early Christians also demonstrated radical compassion for their neighbors.

The most dramatic example of this behavior came when a plague broke out in Caesarea early in the fourth century. While pagans who were still well rushed out of the city, Christians stayed behind to care for the sick and dying often at the expense of their own lives. The early church father Eusebius left this account:

> The evidence of the Christians' zeal and piety was made clear to all the pagans. For example, they alone in such a catastrophic state of affairs gave practical evidence of their sympathy and philanthropy by works. All day long some of them would diligently persevere in performing the last offices for the dying and burying them (for there were countless numbers, and no one to look after them). While others [Christians] gathered together in a single assemblage all who were afflicted by famine throughout the whole city, and would distribute bread to them all. When this became known, people glorified the God of the Christians, and, convinced by the deeds themselves, confessed the Christians alone were truly pious and God-fearing.[10]

This kind of behavior caused the pagan emperor Julian to rail against "the hated Galileans" who "not only feed their own poor, but also ours, welcoming them into their agape." Why was Julian so angry? Because he recognized that the sacrificial compassion of the "Galileans" was dangerous to his dreams of a pagan empire. The willingness of the Christians to set aside their own safety for the sake of their neighbors was the best recruiting tool imaginable. As Romans witnessed the stark difference between Christians and pagans in the midst of the plague, many turned to Christ.

History is replete with such examples. When the early European and American missionaries set sail for Africa they would often pack their coffins with them, all too aware they would likely die of malaria or some other disease and never return. The early results of many of these missions were not promising. But slowly Christian faith took root. Some hundred years ago less than 10 percent of Africans identified as Christians. Today that number stands at 53 percent.[11] Much of the growth can be traced to the dangerous men and women who sacrificed everything to spread the gospel on a distant continent.

## RETHINKING SIN

When I talked with Walker, the brothel-busting detective, I was curious to hear his thoughts about the men who victimized women and girls. Not just the pimps but also the customers, the men who rented the slaves to gratify their desires. While undercover, Walker had to blend in with these men, even pretending to be their friend.

After hearing the heartrending stories of enslaved women and children, I was in no mood for compassion.

"How could you stand to even talk to these perverts?" I asked.

Walker acknowledged the difficulty. "It's easy to hate the men," he said. "A lot of people say, 'These are despicable, disgusting lowlifes.' And they are. But it's easy to forget that we were all slaves and we're set free."

One man confessed to Walker, "You know, I hate my life, and I hate what I do." Walker shook his head sadly as he recounted the conversation to me.

"I realized he is powerless in his enslavement to the desires he's fed through pornography and other means."

I struggled to think of these men as "slaves." But Walker's next words made me even more uncomfortable. He drew parallels between the men he'd met in the sex industry and men in the church.

"So many men within the church are enslaved to vices because they haven't heard, 'There's a far greater adventure, there is far greater pleasure than you'll ever find in the cheap imitations you're seeking out.'"

Walker longs to see men rise up to abolish sex slavery rather than fund it. He urges men, "Use your masculine strength on behalf of the millions of little girls and desperate women who are waiting for you to show up. That's the adventure you're called to. Because we're not doing that, they are trying to find an imitation that fills their need for risk and for danger and for adventure."

Though I struggled to see these perpetrators as victims, I had to concede Walker's point about the nature of sin. It isn't merely about refraining from certain activities; it's about redirecting and redeeming our desires for holy pursuits.

The nineteenth-century Scottish preacher Thomas Chalmers spoke of the "expulsive power of a new affection." For him, conquering sin wasn't a matter of steely resolve; it was best accomplished by replacing sinful affections with holy ones. "A moralist will be unsuccessful in trying to displace his love of the world by reviewing the ills of the world," he preached. "Misplaced affections need to be replaced by the far greater power of the affection of the gospel."[12]

This principle gives us insight into why people indulge in destructive behaviors in the first place. Take, for instance, a middle-aged man who cheats on his wife. Why does he do it? It's not simply because of raging hormones. He had more testosterone in his twenties. It's rarely because he's dissatisfied with his spouse's appearance. In fact, one study found that only 12 percent of cheating men said their mistresses were more physically attractive than their wives.[13] So why would he cheat? Often it's because he's thirsty for transcendence, for adventure. He wants an experience that will lift him, if only temporarily, above the boredom of his mundane, workaday existence. Of course sexual desire plays a role, as does selfishness and lack of self-control. There's no excusing his actions. But at the heart of the act is a legitimate desire that has been twisted into sinful expression. As someone once said, "Every man who knocks on the door of a brothel is really looking for God."

Misguided attempts to grasp for transcendence affect many areas of our lives. Connie Jakab, a Christian writer and activist, lamented the ways women have been reduced to their appearances through messages sent through shows like *Desperate Housewives*. Playing off the word *desperate*, she challenged other women to reimagine their role:

> You weren't created to be *desperate*, you were created to be *dangerous*. You have life-changing impact living inside of you. That's what is going to make you beautiful and vibrant, not another Botox treatment. Dangerous will look good on you. Go try that on for size.[14]

It isn't just sexual sin or self-image problems that are fueled by an undercurrent of misdirected desire. We warn against drug and alcohol abuse, and rightfully so. But it's easy to miss the bigger picture. I believe the primary reason it's wrong to get drunk or high is because of what such experiences replace. They are synthetic forms of transcendence, cheap replacements for encounters with the living God. When the Bible warns against drunkenness, it includes a corresponding command: "Do not get drunk on wine. . . . Instead, be filled with the Spirit" (Eph. 5:18). Why is drunkenness wrong? Because there's a better experience awaiting us—being filled with the Spirit! Our desire for transcendence isn't the problem; satisfying it in destructive ways is. Sin is the result of desires that have been sublimated and sent sideways.

Sin hurts people and ruins relationships. But perhaps the greatest tragedy is what sin keeps us from—the grand adventure of a life lived with and for God.

## DANGEROUS LOVE

Let's get real. You probably won't be martyred in the jungles of Ecuador. Or be called to go to Africa with a coffin in tow. Or storm brothels around the world. You may. But it's more likely that your calling will be right here at home, raising godly children or representing Christ in your workplace. Those, too, are high and holy callings.

Mark Buchanan, a pastor in British Columbia, was approached by a young single mother. She wanted to put her child in foster care because, as she vehemently claimed, "God is calling me to lead the nations in worship, and he wants me to go to Australia and train under Darlene Zschech." Buchanan went on to explain that she had no money, no connection with Darlene Zschech (an Australian worship leader), and no great talent. "Nevertheless," Buchanan wrote, "she was utterly convinced God required this of her."

71

Through a series of questions, Buchanan gently counseled her to stay put. "Today she's now middle-aged, married, raising three children, and lives down the road."[15]

Sometimes the most spiritual thing we can do is stay right where we are (1 Cor. 7:20). But that doesn't mean we don't live radical lives.

This is a challenge for me. I'm an idealistic person. In the past I held something of an either-or mind-set about the Christian life. Either I have to sell everything I own, move to a Third World country, and live in a hut—or stay where I am and live like everyone else. Strange thinking, I know. But if you think God approves of only those with extreme callings, it's easy to throw up your hands and stop trying altogether. We fall prey to what philosophers call "the fallacy of the excluded middle." This refers to flawed thinking that presents only two extremes as plausible options, while ignoring perfectly good choices in the middle.

God may not call you to travel to a distant land or to die for your faith, but you are called to live wholeheartedly for him wherever you are, in whatever you're doing. The specific places and vocations God calls us to are secondary. The important things are whether we walk with him, take risks where we are, and live as threats to the evil around us. The dangerous God is needed as much in an American suburb as a Colombian brothel.

## DRAWN BY DANGER

Historian Joseph Loconte asked, "What is it that makes people build shrines, collect relics, preserve the blood of martyrs, and travel to faraway places to touch the bones of long-dead individuals thought to be close to God?"

Loconte concluded that chalking up these seemingly strange behaviors to superstition isn't satisfying. For him there's something deeper going on:

> Apparently there is something about everyday life—even in our most satisfying moments—that leaves many people anxious for something else. There seems to be a powerful impulse in human nature to connect with a "wondrous, virtuous, transcendent" figure: to be in the presence of God.[16]

In 2013 a zoo in China started receiving complaints about one of its exhibits. As visitors approached the "African lion" cage, they were puzzled to hear barking sounds coming from the creature inside. Turns out the enclosure housed a Tibetan mastiff—a large dog with a thick ring of fur around its neck. Running low on funds, the zoo attempted to pass off the dog as a lion—and visitors weren't happy. "The zoo is absolutely trying to cheat us," one visitor said. "If this works why would people even bother to go to the zoo!"[17] said another. Indeed. No one goes to a zoo to see a dog.

A friend remarked to me, "Everyone's scared of meeting a bear when they're out hiking. But when you go to the zoo, those are the animals that are most popular. It's the dangerous animals everyone wants to see."

It's the same way with God. We may fear a dangerous, transcendent God, but we need him. Desperately. Other deities may suffice for a season. As long as things are going well, smaller and safer gods may keep us happy by promising never to rock the boat.

But the moment we encounter evil, when our lives are overturned by injustice, that's when we need the dangerous God. The one who judges sin and hates evil. It's the same God who rescues us from our lives of quiet desperation. He alone can slake our thirst for transcendence and meaning. In the end, only this God will do.

# SIX
# GOD INCOGNITO

**IN ISAIAH'S VISION GOD IS OBVIOUS, OVERPOWERING.** There's no missing a throne in the sky surrounded by thundering angels. The sting of smoke in your eyes tends to get your attention, as does having a red-hot coal pressed against your lips.

But the truth is God rarely shows up that way. Most of us will never witness such a dramatic display. Not on this side of eternity. The ways God reveals himself to us are more subtle. In fact, most of the time, God is hidden. We don't see clear evidence of him or his activities in our everyday lives. No hand reaches down from the sky to guide us. No audible voice from the heavens tells us what to do. Most of the time he is a stranger simply because he shows up as one.

I discovered this truth in dramatic fashion when I visited an unusual event in one of America's poorest neighborhoods.

## SINGING ON SKID ROW

Every Wednesday night at 7 p.m., Central City Community Church of the Nazarene hosts a karaoke night in the heart of LA's notorious Skid Row. The church opens its doors and stage, turns on a karaoke machine, and invites denizens of the street to be the stars. The event is a community staple, drawing around three hundred people each week. While I was attending seminary in Pasadena, my wife and I had a chance to go and catch the show.

Though we arrived thirty minutes early, a line had already formed, stretching from the front door of the church and around the side of the building. I was a little nervous. We'd never ventured to this part of town. LA's Skid Row is the nation's largest service-dependent ghetto. The forgotten sector of the city is home to some twenty thousand homeless people. Many of the buildings that are not used as service centers are abandoned and boarded. Garbage drifts through the streets. Bodies blanket the sidewalks. Some sleep, while others stare blankly, seemingly oblivious to the incessant wail of sirens.

As we drove in through the dismal surroundings, it was difficult to believe we were still in America—harder still to remember that only minutes away were Hollywood and some of the most expensive shopping in the world. But the concentration of homelessness is no accident. "They just dump them there," I was told. "The police pick up derelicts from all over the city and drop them within a five-block radius." Two weeks earlier I'd seen a disturbing story on the local news. Security cameras outside a Skid Row rescue mission caught a white van pulling up and dropping off an elderly woman in a hospital gown before speeding off.

Once inside the church, the grim reality beyond the walls seemed worlds away. Inside the sanctuary (more an oversized room than a sanctuary) the excitement was tangible. Participants lined up to take the stage and greeted one another warmly with hugs and slaps on the back.

The night opened with a short sermon. "No matter how many times you've blown it, God loves you. You can always start over again," shouted Tony, a barrel-chested pastor. Tony talked about grace and plugged some of ministry's programs for the homeless: weekly support groups, 12-step programs, men's small groups, Bible studies, prayer meetings, and the area's only after-school tutoring program for children affected by homelessness. After Tony preached he began the night with a performance of his own. Then others began to take the stage.

There was no such thing as a solo performance. Everyone sang along or hooted their encouragement. The skill level varied. Some performers were tone-deaf. Others should have been cutting albums. But no matter the talent, the crowd shouted its affirmation. I remember being struck by the stark contrast between the environment and the reality singing shows on TV. No snarky, sarcastic judges—just an incredible warmth and acceptance of everyone, regardless of skill level. It was the anti–*American Idol*.

Midway through the show I made my way over to Tony, who greeted me exactly as he seemed to greet all his parishioners, with a two-fisted handshake and a tug that almost landed me in his arms. Tony was no stranger to the streets. He had pushed a cart through the neighborhood for two years before conquering his drug addiction. No wonder he preached so passionately about second chances.

"Many of the homeless won't come in for church," Tony told me. "But they come for karaoke. When they walk through our door we have an opportunity to meet them. We can get our hands on them, touch them, and connect with them." The ultimate goal of building relationships is restoration. "We want to give them the tools to turn their lives around. We want to see them get off the streets."

Later I talked to one of the other organizers, who raved about the abilities the homeless possess. "The people of Skid Row are very talented," he said. "The karaoke night gives them an opportunity to showcase that talent and build their self-esteem."

After talking with Tony I returned to my seat to witness some of that talent. Four elderly black gentlemen took the stage, and, judging from the excitement of the crowd, I could tell they'd done this before. Their voices were low and full of gravel.

> *There have been times when the times were so hard*
> *But somehow, some way I'd made it through . . .* [1]

After their performance, the crowd roared for an encore. They obliged before passing the microphone over to a young woman who sang the R. Kelly pop song, "I Believe I Can Fly." I had heard the song before, yet in that context the words had new meaning.

> *I used to think that I could not go on.*
> *And life was nothing but an awful song.*
> *But now I know the meaning of true love.*
> *I'm leaning on the everlasting arms.* [2]

Her voice was powerful. She paused before launching into the chorus, "I believe I can fly." Throughout the room eyes pinched shut and hands began to rise.

> *I believe I can touch the sky.*
> *I think about it every night and day.*
> *Spread my wings and fly away.*[3]

I looked out across the audience. *This isn't a concert anymore,* I thought. *This is a worship service.*

Midway through the show, Tony returned to the stage for an impromptu altar call. "If you need prayer tonight, I want you to join me at the back." A few people slipped out of their chairs, but Tony wasn't satisfied. He spotted other subjects in need of prayer. Their reluctance was no obstacle for Tony—he pulled them right out of their chairs and playfully coaxed them to the back where a small team encircled each person for a time of spirited petition.

As the prayer intermission wrapped up, the performances resumed. The next singer was breathtaking—a veritable Beyoncé—with perfect pitch and soaring range. She improvised lyrics and dazzled the crowd with her vocal gymnastics. As the song concluded, she wandered from the teleprompter and paced back and forth in front of the crowd.

> *He's helped me, Jesus, yes he has. I don't know what you're going*
> *    through.*
> *But I want to encourage you—he went through it too.*
> *Don't give up don't give in. With Jesus we can win.*

On her last crescendo, the crowd spontaneously surged forward. People piled onstage. The night concluded with every man, woman, and child singing and dancing.

I'd come to the event curious and a little scared. I was prepared to face the poverty of others, but not my own. And I certainly didn't expect to encounter such a visible manifestation of God's presence. But there amid the most hopeless and impoverished people in all of Los Angeles, it was unmistakable. I was blindsided by God in the last place you'd expect to find him.

## HIDDEN GOD

When theologians talk about the "hiddenness of God," they treat it as a major problem. It's something to overcome or explain, like the age-old problem of evil. Atheists use it to score rhetorical points in debates. "If God exists," they say, "why doesn't he just show himself?"

One skeptic I heard speak was kind enough to offer God a simple way to prove his existence. God could simply arrange the stars of the night sky to spell out a message in Hebrew.

I chuckled at the idea. The suggestion reminded me of another odd assurance sought by a friend. "I wish God would speak to me in a Russian accent," he joked. "Then I could be sure the voice I heard wasn't mine."

It isn't only skeptics troubled by God's hiddenness. C. S. Lewis once said, "The 'hiddenness' of God perhaps presses most painfully on those who are in another way nearest to Him."[4]

I think I know what Lewis meant. As believers we feel more entitled to evidence of God's existence and love. Like the elder brother in the parable of the prodigal son, we've faithfully served our heavenly Father. Shouldn't we receive tangible assurances in return?

But God's presence isn't always assuring. As we have seen, the kind of direct contact we crave can bring more terror than tranquility. Encounters of the Isaiah 6 variety are rare. And frankly, I'm grateful they are. We think of God's hiddenness as a challenge to our faith, and it is. It is also a sort of blessing, an act of mercy from a God who shelters our fragile bodies from the full weight of his glory.

Still, this hiddenness haunts us. The pastor of a church I attended grappled openly with his doubts. I remember him raising his hands heavenward. "God, I don't need a burning bush," he cried. "A flaming dandelion would do!"

## DIVINE DISGUISES

When Carly Fleischmann was two, her parents noticed that she was missing key developmental milestones. Unlike her twin sister, Carly was unable to sit up or walk. But that's not what her family found most devastating. As the years passed, it became obvious Carly would never be able to communicate.

Carly was diagnosed with autism. Upon the diagnosis, Carly's parents enrolled her in intensive therapy. Multiple therapists worked with her for up to sixty hours per week. Her progress was painfully slow. She couldn't speak, not one word. And her

odd behaviors—tantrums, drooling, hand flapping, head bang-
ing, fecal smearing, and constant rocking—remained stubbornly
in place.

Then, a miracle. One day Carly unexpectedly walked over
to an open laptop and tapped out a message: "hurt." Prompted
by a therapist to keep typing, she spelled out another word:
"help."

Her parents had a hard time believing the news. "Knowing
this child for over ten years and never seeing her type a thing,
of course you're going to be skeptical," her father told the TV
show *20/20*. The other therapists were incredulous too. And to
everyone's frustration, Carly wouldn't type again.

That is, until a little pressure was applied. If Carly wanted
anything, she would have to type. "Oh, she had to work for it,"
recalled Nicole Walton-Allen, a clinical psychologist who led
Carly's therapy program. "If she wanted information, if she wanted
to go somewhere, she would have to type. By herself."

The strategy paid off. After a few months, Carly started typing for others. And what she had to say amazed people. Locked
within her broken body was a bright, normal girl. "I am autistic,
but that's not who I am," Carly wrote. "Take time to know me,
before you judge me. I am cute, funny, and like to have fun."

Her newfound ability to communicate also shed light on
her baffling condition. Why did she bang her head? Now Carly
could explain:

Because if I don't, it feels like my body is going to explode.
It's just like when you shake a can of Coke. If I could stop it I
would, but it's not like turning a switch off.

Why do autistic children cover their ears, flap their hands, and rock?

> It's a way for us to drown out all sensory input that over-loads us all at once. Our brains are wired differently. We take in many sounds and conversations at once. I take over a thousand pictures of a person's face when I look at them. That's why we have a hard time looking at people.

Today Carly communicates with people all over the world. She has written a book and has thousands of fans on Facebook and Twitter. Still, no one appreciates her ability to communicate more than her family members. Her dad shakes his head as he reflects on the experience. "Two years we've been communicating, and every time there's a little bit of that sense of awe."[5]

I love Carly's story. It's an inspiring account of a young girl's determination and courage as well as a powerful testament to her family's tenacious love.

It also reminds me of the way God chooses to be present in our world. Like Carly's intelligence, God's presence is not always apparent. At first glance you're almost sure to miss it. In fact, looking for God in our world can feel a little like searching for signs of intelligence in the flailing of an autistic child. When you look at the perplexing events unfolding around us, not to mention the brutal and tragic ones, God seems very far away indeed.

And yet he is there.

Like Carly's keen mind was obscured by her spasmodic body movements, God's presence is often hidden beneath the turbulent and seemingly haphazard happenings of our lives. Ancient cosmology placed God's home in the sky. But I've found it as helpful to think of God beneath the surface of things, waiting to emerge in unexpected ways.

## PERFECT STRANGERS

For the most part, these appearances are decidedly understated. Rather than coming in the wind, an earthquake, or a fire, God inhabits a whisper. He forgoes the palace of Caesar for the confines of the virgin's womb. He rides, not a royal steed, but a donkey. He prefers the role of suffering servant to that of a conquering king. In other words, when God does show up, he's usually well disguised.

In Genesis 18, the Lord appeared to Abraham in the form of three travelers. Abraham insisted they stop in his tent to eat and rest, and they did. During dinner they dropped a bombshell: Abraham's elderly wife, Sarah, would bear a child.

Jacob, too, had a divine encounter. While camping by the Jabbok River, he had a twilight wrestling match with a stranger. The fight went all night till at last the mysterious man agreed to bless Jacob. The stranger dislocated Jacob's hip and renamed Jacob "Israel." After the struggle, Jacob realized the stranger's identity. He limped toward the sunrise overawed. "I saw God face to face, and yet my life was spared" (Gen. 32:30).

Instances of divine disguise are not limited to the Old Testament. In the gospel of Luke, Jesus appeared disguised on the road to Emmaus. The story comes on the heels of the crucifixion as two of Jesus' disciples walked to the village of Emmaus from Jerusalem.

We are told nothing about these disciples, other than that one of them was named Cleopas. What we do know is their state of mind. They're dejected, disheartened. "They stood still, their faces downcast," Luke wrote (24:17). It's easy to see why. Jesus, their leader and friend, the one they believed "was going to redeem Israel," had been murdered. The movement was over. Their hope was gone. And they were afraid. With their leader executed they were probably leaving Jerusalem because it was no longer safe for them there. But there's more than fear at work here. You can hear it in their voices. Pangs of disappointment, confusion, doubt, unfulfilled longing. "We had hoped that he was the one . . ." (v. 21).

If anyone could have used an undeniable divine visitation, it was these two. Yet that's not what they received. Instead, a stranger approached and then walked alongside them. Ironies abound. The "stranger" was Jesus, the very one whose death they were mourning. Cleopas informed Jesus about the events of the preceding days when, of course, no one knew better than Jesus what had transpired.

Even when Jesus broke his silence, explaining how Scripture shows how the Messiah must suffer, the disciples failed to understand who he was. They only recognized him later, when Jesus, their guest, became the host and broke bread in their midst. The moment they recognized him, he vanished.

## SECRET IDENTITIES

Odd as the story is, it fits the pattern we see in Scripture. We don't know why Jesus masks his identity. We can't say why, even when the disciples recognize him, he suddenly disappears. Nor for that matter, do we know why the Lord visited Abraham in the form of three travelers or why God picked a late-night fight with Jacob. The truth is that God often chooses to reveal himself in ways that are hard to understand, easy to miss, and tempting to deny. Malcolm Muggeridge put it this way: "The prophets, when they appear on our earthly scene, are rarely as expected. A king is awaited, and there is a birth in a manger. The venerable, the bearded, the portentous are usually spurious."[6]

The incarnation (the teaching that God became flesh) is the best example. Many struggle with the notion that God's greatest revelation came in the form of a Jewish baby, born to a teenager, in a barn. Talk about being hidden!

Even during his ministry, Jesus' identity was veiled to most. Though he performed miracles and amazed crowds with his teaching, he was less than forthcoming about who he was. He never explicitly claimed to be the Messiah. Instead he preferred to have others confess his identity. Even then he warned them from telling others (Mark 8:29–30).

The way Jesus referred to himself was similarly modest. He called himself the "Son of Man," a title he used more than any other. In the language of the day "Son of Man" simply meant "human." It may have had another meaning too.

The prophet Daniel had a vision in which he described seeing "one like a son of man" (7:13). God approached this mysterious person and gave him "authority, glory and sovereign power" (v. 14). By calling himself the "Son of Man" Jesus linked his identity to this exalted figure. Yet even in asserting this lofty identity, Jesus did so indirectly. He used allusion and echo, ensuring that his identity would remain obscured to all but the most sincere seekers.

Author Philip Yancey summed it up well:

> Jesus himself, when challenged, did not offer airtight proofs of his identity. He dropped clues here and there, to be sure, but he also said, after appealing to the evidence, "Blessed is he who takes no offense at me." It occurs to me that all the contorted theories about Jesus that have been spontaneously generating since the day of his death merely confirm the awesome risk God took when he stretched himself out on the dissection table—a risk he seemed to welcome. Examine me. Test me. You decide.[7]

Don't get me wrong. Jesus spoke the truth in ways people could understand. He provided supernatural evidence of his identity. He repeatedly affirmed that he was the Messiah. But he knew that ultimately people would accept or reject him based on the condition of their hearts and the inner calling of his Father. "My sheep hear my voice," he said (John 10:27 NKJV). He was never anxious to prove who he was.

None of this disturbs me, truthfully. I'll take a humble Messiah over a ham-fisted self-promoter any day. What troubles me is this: while Jesus seemed willing to risk being overlooked and undervalued, I am not. When criticized, I get defensive. When insulted, my tendency is to lash out. All too often I put my own sinful twist on the Golden Rule and do to others exactly what they have done to me. But if Jesus, the "express image" of the Father (Heb. 1:3 NKJV), God in the flesh, didn't feel the need to defend himself, why should I? If Jesus was comfortable as a stranger in this world, shouldn't I be too?

The way Jesus communicated his identity holds an important lesson for how we should think about ours. The Bible says our true identities are "hidden with Christ in God" (Col. 3:3). We are citizens of a kingdom that Jesus said is "not of this world" (John 18:36). When we grasp this reality, everything changes. When people reject us, we're hurt, but not devastated. Our emotions are not tethered to our latest successes or failures. We don't clamor for accolades. We are known by God, so we're willing to embrace obscurity. We trust the Lord to vindicate us, so we're free to turn the other cheek. We're willing to be misunderstood and even mocked because we are loved by our Father in heaven. If the world doesn't recognize us, we are not fazed. After all, we are followers of the Great Stranger.

We also know that what is hidden now will not be hidden forever. Ultimately God will pull back the curtain to reveal his identity and reward his servants.

## THE BIG REVEAL

My wife and I enjoy watching *Undercover Boss*. This reality TV show portrays what happens when a hidden identity is revealed. The show follows corporate executives as they work undercover at entry-level positions in the very companies they lead. The bosses report for work in disguise, with fake names and fictitious backstories. Each undercover boss is assigned an employee to train him or her. As they work together, a camera catches the action. It's amusing to watch CEOs trying to flip burgers, load crates, and clean toilets. But the show's most moving moments come as the disguised bosses become acquainted with the professional and personal problems of their employees.

After a week of working undercover, the executives return to their old lives. Each episode ends with dedicated employees being summoned to corporate headquarters, where they are rewarded with gifts and promotions. Again they meet the boss, but this time things are different. Instead of donning work clothes, the boss wears an expensive suit. Rather than working a menial job, the boss sits behind a large desk in a spacious office. The employee discovers the person whom they thought was a low-level employee was actually a wealthy executive. The one to whom they gave orders was the one in charge all along.

The revelation reduces many to tears. One employee, a sweet-spirited truck driver from Kazakhstan, exclaimed, "Big boss comes to the plain worker. I could not believe that was happened!"[8]

I think that's a great picture of the Christian story. If history were an episode of *Undercover Boss*, right now we'd be in the middle of the show. At this stage God is hidden. He only shows up in disguise. And what disguises he wears! He comes to us as the homeless woman singing karaoke, the challenging coworker, the friend in need, or your spouse or children. And the beautiful and terrifying truth is that how we respond to him in these forms has eternal significance.

We also know that God has a surprise planned, that this story has a twist. One day he will call his servants to his heavenly headquarters to reward them and unveil his full identity. On that day I wonder if we will gasp as we discover the ways he was present in our world. *That was you! It was really you? The Big Boss comes to plain workers?*

In the meantime, it's important to look for him in the world. And remember, he's still the God of Isaiah 6. His throne is still exalted. Smoke still fills the temple. The seraphim still cry holy. No matter the disguises he wears.

# PART TWO
# DIVINE EMBRACE

# SEVEN

# LOVING A LION

**WE WERE HOPING FOR A GOOD LOOK AT THE LIONS.**

On our first visit to the local zoo the lions were shy, hanging toward the back of their enclosure or lounging on high, rocky ledges.

This time my wife and I wanted a closer look. And not just for us. Our infant son had a passion for the regal beasts. At least that's what we inferred from his behavior. Each time he spotted a lion in one of his children's books, he would smile and let out a diminutive roar. Now, we hoped, he would get to see the real thing.

It was a rainy day. As we pushed his stroller along the path leading to the Big Cats area, we worried the rain might send the lions into hiding. When we arrived at the enclosure, our fears were confirmed—no lions. We leaned against the fence. It was no more than five feet tall, hardly an obstacle for the massive felines. A giant moat dug just beyond the fence provided the real protection. We scanned the far bank of the moat, looked up in the trees, and searched the stone slabs for slumbering cats. Nothing. Had they been moved for some reason?

There was one other place to check. If you continued down the path, you came upon a large, Plexiglas window with a side view of the enclosure. When we rounded the corner, we were greeted by an incredible sight: the lion and lioness sitting mere feet away.

As we approached, the male lifted his great head from the ground. With a mighty yawn, he raised himself to full height and stepped toward us. I could have extended my arm and touched him were it not for the safety glass, which fogged up each time he exhaled. We figured he must have been about nine feet long and around five hundred pounds. His enormous mane bounced with the breeze but his head remained still. For a good minute he looked directly at us, as if in a trance.

Our son was silent. Not a peep, let alone a roar. Did he know this was a real lion? Perhaps he failed to identify the monster before us with the caricatures of his picture books. Or maybe, like us, he was overawed.

Just then a group of tourists skipped up beside us. Their arrival seemed to break the lion's reverie. He started to pace back and forth, agitated. The tourists held up smartphones to snap pictures and rapped on the glass trying to get the creature's attention. A boy of about twelve, frustrated the lion wouldn't turn in his direction, slammed his palm against the glass. "Over here, dummy!" he shouted.

Until then, it had been a solemn, almost sacred, moment. Standing before the lion produced a strange mix of emotions. Initially I felt fear. I knew I was safe, but there was still an involuntary fear response to being in close proximity to one of nature's greatest killing machines. At the same time, it was exhilarating.

I had never been so close to a lion. There is something deeply affecting about being in the presence of such a formidable creature.

After a few minutes, the tourists moved along to the next exhibit. The lion seemed to calm down, and we enjoyed more time simply marveling at the majestic animal.

That whole weekend I couldn't stop thinking about the experience. Why did my encounter with the lion leave such an impact? It wasn't because he was cute and cuddly. No, it was because he was powerful and dangerous. It was precisely those fearsome qualities that made being near him so special. It's the same reason people go on safaris or whale-watching ventures or (for the truly intrepid) cage diving to get close to great white sharks. It's why we tell our children stories about dragons then tuck them into bed clutching stuffed bears. We crave the presence of something great and terrible.

There's a similar dynamic with God. It's his greatness and glory that make his presence meaningful. In fact, only when we glimpse his splendor and strangeness will we awaken to the significance of his nearness.

So far we have focused on God's transcendence, those attributes that place him above and beyond his creation. Isaiah's vision of the Lord exalted in the temple highlights this attribute, as does the dramatic appearance on Mount Sinai. We've seen God as "the other," as dangerous, a holy consuming fire. We've observed the lion from afar.

But in addition to God's transcendence, the Bible portrays God as *immanent*, a word that literally means "to be within" or "near."[1] We see this reality repeatedly in Scripture. The God of the Bible is not some distant deity, watching humanity from afar with cool indifference. He's a restless revealer who longs to make his presence known.

The Old Testament is filled with eruptions of divine love. Consider Zephaniah 3:17: "The LORD your God is in your midst, / a mighty one who will save; / he will rejoice over you with gladness; / he will quiet you by his love; / he will exult over you with loud singing" (ESV). The Bible's most popular verse begins with the words, "For God so loved the world" (John 3:16).

## A BEAUTIFUL BALANCE

Most religions tend to emphasize either God's transcendence or his immanence.

In Islam, for instance, Allah is utterly transcendent. And this transcendence is guarded zealously. Representations of the divine are strictly forbidden, as are human comparisons. The only unpardonable sin mentioned in the Qur'an is to attribute divinity to a created entity. Muslims believe God has revealed himself through the prophets, but in Islamic thought, God is ultimately unknowable.

In the medieval era, some Islamic scholars developed a theology that proposed speaking of Allah only in double negatives.[2] Rather than saying, "Allah is merciful," they would say, "Allah is not unmerciful." They felt using such negations was necessary to describe an inscrutable God. Making positive affirmations about Allah was going too far, they decided. Mere mortals could only hope to say what *isn't* true of him.

Most Eastern belief systems, on the other hand, stress divine immanence. In Hinduism, there is no significant distinction between god and the material world. Hindus worship many gods, yet all are seen as manifestations of Brahman, the supreme deity. Hindus see no essential difference between Brahman and the universe. As the Upanishads, the Hindu scriptures, say, "This whole universe is Brahman, from Brahman to a clod of earth."[3] The divine is utterly immanent.

Christianity is unique. It maintains that God is both transcendent *and* immanent. We believe God is above and beyond the physical world, and present within it. Mysterious but knowable. The Bible is the story of how the transcendent God has been revealed. Jesus tells his disciples they have been "given to know the mysteries of the kingdom of God" (Luke 8:10 NKJV). Paul uses the Greek word *mystārion*—from which we get our word *mystery*—twenty times in the New Testament. But the word is always used to point to the joyous fact that God has made his mysteries known in Jesus Christ. That's the good news—God hasn't left us in the dark but has revealed his *mystārion* in the person of his Son. Scholars Steven Boyer and Christopher Hall explained that the most common usage of the word *mystery* in the Bible is not to denote "a puzzle to solve or a question to answer." Rather, the word speaks of "a marvelous plan or purpose that God has revealed for creation."[4]

We also believe that God is present in our world, but not part of it. If the earth were destroyed, God would be grieved but not diminished. Though he reveals himself through creation, he is independent of it. Still, his immanence is real. God ceaselessly reveals his character in and through the world. It's a point made time and again in Scripture. "The heavens declare the glory of God," the psalmist declared. "The skies proclaim the work of his hands. / Day after day they pour forth speech; / night after night they reveal knowledge" (Ps. 19:1–2). A. W. Tozer wrote of the pervasiveness of God's immanence in the Bible:

> Those passages supporting this truth are so plain that it would take considerable effort to misunderstand them. They declare that God is imminent in His creation, that there is no place in heaven or earth or hell where men may hide from His presence. They teach that God is at once far off and near.[5]

The writers of Scripture seem quite comfortable placing God's transcendence and immanence side by side. Often we glimpse both qualities squeezed into the same passage.

When Paul spoke with the Greek philosophers in Athens, he underscored God's transcendence: "The God who made the world and everything in it is the Lord of heaven and earth and does not live in temples built by human hands." In the same speech he spoke of God's immanence: ". . . though he is not far from any one of us. 'For in him we live and move and have our being'" (Acts 17:24–28).

In Isaiah, depictions of God's might and sovereignty give way to tender descriptions of his nearness and love:

> *See, the Sovereign LORD comes with power,*
> *and he rules with a mighty arm.*
> *See, his reward is with him,*
> *and his recompense accompanies him.*
> *He tends his flock like a shepherd:*
> *He gathers the lambs in his arms*
> *and carries them close to his heart;*
> *he gently leads those that have young. (40:10–11)*

In Jeremiah, God speaks of both his transcendence and immanence:

> *"Am I only a God nearby,"*
> *declares the LORD,*
> *"and not a God far away?*
> *Can anyone hide in secret places*
> *so that I cannot see him?"*
> *declares the LORD.*
> *"Do not I fill heaven and earth?"*
> *declares the LORD. (23:23–24)*

This paradox is present in God's very name. When the Lord commanded Moses to go to Egypt and lead the Israelites out of slavery, Moses sought assurances.

Moses said to God, "Suppose I go to the Israelites and say to them, 'The God of your fathers has sent me to you,' and they ask me, 'What is his name?' Then what shall I tell them?" (Ex. 3:13)

God's response seems cryptic:

God said to Moses, "I AM WHO I AM. This is what you are to say to the Israelites: 'I AM has sent me to you.'" (v. 14)

"I AM" doesn't seem like a very clear answer to Moses' question. The alternate reading provided by some Bibles—"I will be what I will be"—does little to clarify the matter. Yet most scholars see an assurance of God's presence in this response, a sign of "the reality of God's active, dynamic presence."[6] At the same time, God's response amounts to an "evasion of the questioner's intent," according to scholar Michael P. Knowles.

> Moses' desire to know the name of God amounts to a bid for control, an attempt to gain some degree of power over this terrifyingly intrusive deity. In the world of Moses' day, to know someone's name is to know what is most true about that person; to know the name of your god grants access to the hidden identity, nature, and power of that god. If you know and can call on the name of that god, you have that god in your power.[7]

If Moses was looking for this kind of control, God's response makes perfect sense. "I AM" is a sovereign assertion of identity. It's a declaration of being that seeks no external validation. It's as if God was saying, "I'm above your categories and your control. I don't answer to you. I don't have to explain myself or justify my existence; I just am." As Knowles put it, the name is "self-authenticating, not subject to limitation or control by those who call upon it, despite Moses' fervent wish to do just that."[8]

The passage dramatically highlights God's nearness and distinctiveness, his immanence and transcendence.

## IDENTITY ISSUES

Maybe you find talk of God's transcendence a little intimidating. It's not that you deny God's greatness. In fact, you know it all too well. For you, the fear of the Lord comes naturally.

God's holiness makes perfect sense; it's his love you struggle to accept.

Or perhaps you find yourself on the other side of the equation. You readily accept God's nearness and love but balk at his transcendence. God's love and mercy warm your heart, but talk of divine holiness makes you uneasy.

Whatever view of God you gravitate toward, I want to encourage you to resist the urge to collapse one side of the paradox. God is loving and holy, beyond our world and yet powerfully present within it.

We may think we're not vulnerable to either extreme. If we have even a passing familiarity with Scripture, we're likely to acknowledge that God is both holy and loving. But there's a strong tendency to shortchange either his holiness or his love, downplaying one attribute for the sake of the other. We say, "Yes, God is holy, but . . ." or "Yes, God is loving, but . . ." We may concede that God is love, yet still feel like he's out to get us, waiting for us to mess up so he can drop the divine hammer. Or we might pay lip service to God's justice but inwardly feel that he's so filled with love that he's not all that concerned with holiness.

If you're the first kind of person, stay tuned. The second half of this book is all about God's nearness and love. Fearing the Lord is essential, but we must also internalize the reality of his love. An all-powerful but unloving god can only inspire fear. A deity devoid of love may elicit awe, but never affection. We would only flee this god or serve him cringingly, taking ever-greater precautions to avoid provoking his wrath.

If you're the second type of person, I want to challenge you. Don't lose sight of God's holiness and power. Those very qualities make his love significant. Without a healthy respect for God's greatness, his affection loses value.

Consider the following example—this time from the human realm. If you received a thoughtful card from a friend or family member, I'm guessing you'd appreciate it. You might even display the card on your desk or fridge for a week or two. But after a while, it would likely wind up in the recycle bin and fade from memory. A kind gesture, but nothing monumental.

Now imagine that same scenario, but with a twist. Instead of receiving the card from a friend or family member, it comes from the president of the United States. It's handwritten and signed by the president himself. Suddenly whether you agree with the president's politics doesn't matter so much. You feel honored that the most powerful person in the country thought of you. Rather than slapping the card on your fridge for a week or two, you show it to all your friends—and keep it forever. Maybe you even have it framed.

You may never receive such a letter from the president (I'm still waiting for mine), but the imaginary situation illustrates a real-life principle. The identity of the giver matters. And not just when we're talking about getting cards from important people. It is far more important when it comes to receiving love from a holy God. That's why it's essential we have a healthy respect for God's greatness. The affection of a familiar, buddy deity is one thing; the love of the Lord of heaven and earth, the one who dwells in unapproachable light, is something else entirely. As Francis Chan wrote, "The fact that a holy, eternal, all-knowing, all-powerful, merciful, fair, and just God loves you is nothing short of astonishing."[9]

God's immanence doesn't diminish his transcendence. To

say that God is both transcendent and immanent is not like saying he is big and small. Transcendence is an attribute of God. Immanence, strictly speaking, is not. God's immanence is relational; it doesn't reflect the substance of his nature.[10] God's immanence merely means that the great and holy God has come near. In fact, his transcendence necessitates his immanence. Since his full presence would only overwhelm us, he must reveal himself in more subtle and indirect ways.

Philip Yancey wrote about the challenges of trying to maintain a saltwater aquarium. In addition to running a portable laboratory to maintain precise levels of ammonia content and nitrate levels, he had to constantly supply the fish with vitamins, antibiotics, enzymes, and drugs. Yancey jokingly remarked, "You would think, in view of all the energy expended on their behalf that my fish would at least be grateful." But, of course, the fish showed no signs of appreciation. Quite the opposite, in fact.

> Every time my shadow loomed above the tank they dove for cover into the nearest shell. They showed me one "emotion" only: fear. Although I opened the lid and dropped in food on a regular schedule, three times a day, they responded to each visit as a sure sign of my designs to torture them. I could not convince them of my true concern. To my fish I was a deity. I was too large for them, my actions, too incomprehensible. My acts of mercy they saw as cruelty; my attempts at healing they viewed as destruction. To change their perceptions, I began to see, would require a form of incarnation. I would have to become a fish and "speak to them in a language they could understand."[11]

Yancey is right. God's full glory would be devastating to us. So in order to communicate his love, he became one of us. But we should never let the fact that God took on flesh trick us into thinking he's on par with humanity. In Psalm 50:21 God rebuked mortals for thinking "I was exactly like you," and he declared in Isaiah, "For my thoughts are not your thoughts, / neither are your ways my ways" (55:8).

It's crucial we keep this reality in sight. Only when we gain a proper understanding of God's identity can we begin to appreciate the implications of his love. As we move into an exploration of God's intimacy, let's not lose sight of whom we are speaking.

# EIGHT
# TENACITY AND TENDERNESS

**WE'VE PROVEN OURSELVES UNWORTHY OF GOD'S LOVE.**

We routinely deny, reject, and ignore him. We rebel, hide, lie, cheat, manipulate, you name it. And, yes, there has been physical abuse (though we knew not what we did).

Not to be glib about it, but if we saw a friend being mistreated by a partner this way we'd say: "She's in a bad relationship." We see all the signs. Neglect. Insults. Selfishness.

We might even urge our friend to get out. Maybe she can't see what her partner is doing to her. *You don't have to put up with this. It won't change. You deserve better.*

But God isn't like one of our friends living in denial about a bad relationship. God is all too aware of our sinful behaviors. Yet he refuses to abandon the relationship. He keeps fighting to make it work, even when it kills him.

Sometimes I marvel at the fact that God loves us at all. Does it strike you as somewhat absurd that the Creator of the cosmos desires intimacy with you and me? Does it seem odd that God Almighty loves lowly humans, much less became one?

And it gets stranger. The Bible tells us that God sent his Son to die for us while we were "still sinners" and "God's enemies" (Rom. 5:8, 10). The preemptive act of love is staggering in itself. But it absolutely amazes me that he continues to love us, even as we continue sinning. That he keeps calling us children even when we keep acting like his enemies. To me, that's the true wonder: that God hangs on to us for dear life and keeps loving us despite our failings and unfaithfulness.

In the first half of the book, we examined our tendency to shrink God down to our size. We looked at some of the subtle ways—and not-so-subtle ways—we try to tame the Almighty by ignoring his holiness. But we have another tendency, one that's perhaps just as dangerous: to tame his love. We take the infinite, divine love described in Scripture and place limits on it. We make it reasonable. We project our own faltering brand of affections heavenward and assume God's love is as flawed as ours. Even as we pay lip service to God's boundless mercy, we tabulate our shortcomings and wonder whether we've exhausted his grace. Thankfully, Scripture teems with beautiful correctives to this mentality.

## MARRIED TO A WHORE

If you're offended by my characterization of God's relationship with humanity, don't read the book of Hosea. It contains a much less favorable portrayal. Exasperated by Israel's unfaithfulness, God gave the prophet Hosea a bizarre command: "Go, marry a promiscuous woman and have children with her" (1:2).

"Promiscuous" is really a modern spin. The Hebrew word used here is *zânûwn*, which literally means "whoredom."[1] A more literal rendering would read, "Go marry a hooker." This isn't just a loose woman with a bit of a past. God told Hosea to marry a woman who got paid to have sex with random men, and did so night after night.

Why did God commission such a thing? The marriage was meant to embody Israel's spiritual infidelity to Yahweh: "For like an adulterous wife this land is guilty of unfaithfulness to the LORD" (1:2).

We can only imagine what Hosea's peers made of this odd union. The holy man and the whore. The prophet and the prostitute. No doubt there was head shaking and finger pointing, whispering and snickering. Hosea's friends must have tried convincing him to ditch her, and his enemies must have used it to destroy his reputation. Perhaps parents shielded their children as Hosea and his wife walked by. In the family-based society of ancient Israel, I'm sure marrying a prostitute wasn't exactly a résumé-builder, especially for a man of God.

But Hosea's outward shame likely paled in comparison to his inward agony. After the marriage, Hosea's wife, Gomer, continued to be unfaithful, at one point abandoning Hosea and her children to live with another man. God commanded Hosea to pursue her and take her back (Hos. 3:1–3). Hosea's love for his unfaithful wife mirrors God's love for unfaithful Israel. With each act of adultery, it was as if God was saying to Hosea, to Israel, "See, *that's* how it feels. That's what it's like to see your beloved in the arms of strangers. That's the pain of being betrayed again and again and again."

On top of this, God commanded Hosea to give their children symbolic names. The first child was named Jezreel, after the site of an ancient massacre. Jezreel was where Jehu, king of Israel, had engineered the slaughter of Ahab's descendants. By Hosea's time, it had become synonymous with God's judgment. The second child born to Gomer was named Lo-Ruhamah, which means, "not loved." The third was dubbed Lo-Ammi, meaning "not my people."

Unsurprisingly, the prophecies that followed were scathing and pain-filled. God, the spurned lover, lashed out at his unfaithful people. "I will punish her for the days / she burned incense to the Baals; / she decked herself with rings and jewelry, / and went after her lovers, / but me she forgot" (2:13).

Yet promises of restoration came on the heels of judgment. Already in chapter 2, signs of redemption began to appear. "I will lead her into the wilderness / and speak tenderly to her" (v. 14). Though incensed by his people's unfaithfulness, God is still Israel's true lover, her husband. "'In that day,' declares the LORD, / 'you will call me 'my husband'" (v. 16). Even the curses foretold by the names of Gomer's children would someday be reversed.

> *I will show my love to the one I called "Not my loved one."*
> *I will say to those called "Not my people," "You are my people";*
> *and they will say, "You are my God." (v. 23)*

It's a familiar story line. God's wrath burns bright, revealing Israel's iniquities. He announces judgment and often carries it out. But then a strange thing happens, sometimes smack-dab in the middle of white-hot denunciations: God circles back to mercy. After he has judged his nation, he will pursue and restore her.

> *How can I give you up, Ephraim?*
> *How can I hand you over, Israel?*
> *How can I treat you like Admah?*
> *How can I make you like Zeboyim?*
> *My heart is changed within me;*
> *all my compassion is aroused. (11:8)*

His great love absorbs the offense. Israel is unfaithful yet they are still his—and God refuses to let go. "I have loved you with an everlasting love" (Jer. 31:3).

This is the love that transforms us.

## PASSIONATE PURSUIT

In the 2008 film *Taken*, Liam Neeson plays Bryan Mills, a retired CIA operative who tracks down his teenage daughter after she's kidnapped by human traffickers while vacationing in France. In the moments after his daughter is taken, Mills speaks to one of her abductors on the phone. "I will look for you," he says, "I *will* find you, and I *will* kill you."[2]

The kidnappers do not heed the warning, and as is wont to happen in an action movie, Mills makes good on his promise. No barrier deters him: not government red tape, language barriers, or the multimillion-dollar criminal enterprise holding his daughter captive. Though he's injured and nearly killed, his determination never wavers.

Finally he finds his daughter on a yacht, sold as a prostitute to a wealthy sheikh. After rescuing her, she collapses into her father's arms. "Daddy," she sobs, "you came for me!" He responds, "I told you I would."

It's a gritty, violent film. Mills is a wrecking ball, using his CIA training to dispatch thugs and pimps with brutal efficiency. And yet, for some reason, Mills's character reminds me of God. Not in the particulars of his story, of course. Yet in his single-minded pursuit to save his daughter, I glimpse something of the divine determination we see in Scripture. God comes after us tenaciously, almost recklessly. No obstacle is too great, no cost too high. Like the father in the film, he will endure any hardship to have us back.

The Bible is the record of that passionate pursuit. In story after story, we see God's relentless quest to restore intimacy with his estranged children. "God always has a plan B," the expression goes. But judging from what we see in Scripture, he also seems to have plans C, D, and E. Missionary Lesslie Newbigin described the Bible as "the story of God's tireless, loving, wrathful, inexhaustible patience with the human family, and of our unbelief, blindness, disobedience."[3] We see this pattern from the very beginning.

In the garden of Eden, Adam and Eve enjoyed a close relationship with their Creator. Genesis describes God visiting the garden during "the cool of the day" (3:8), suggesting the sinless couple walked and talked with God. But we all know what happened next. Sin interfered, and they were banished from the garden. The relationship was broken. Intimacy was lost.

As humans increased in number, so did wickedness. It got so bad, we're told that "every inclination of the thoughts of the human heart was only evil all the time" (Gen. 6:5). In a rare moment of divine remorse, God wondered why he created humanity at all. He poured out his wrath, literally, by flooding the earth. But he didn't give up on humanity. There was still one righteous man, Noah. God spared him and his family by instructing them to build an ark. When the waters receded, God made a covenant with Noah and his children. Never again, he promised, would he judge the earth by covering it with water (Gen. 9:11). Echoing the language of Genesis, God commanded Noah and his children, "Be fruitful and increase in number and fill the earth" (v. 1). It's the biggest do-over of all time.

But history repeats itself, and the covenant with God was soon forgotten. A mere two chapters later we see people uniting to build a Mesopotamian temple tower "that reaches to the heavens" (11:4). God frustrated their plans and scattered them, but he had not given up on humanity.

In Genesis 12 God appeared to an old pagan nomad named Abram. He made the childless senior an outrageous promise: "I will make you into a great nation" (v. 2). "I will make your descendants as numerous as the stars in the sky" (Gen. 26:4).

In subsequent generations, as this great nation began to grow, God interacted with them, teaching them his ways and revealing his character. He liberated them from Egypt and led them to Mount Sinai, where he gave them his law. The commandments of this law are many and meticulous, but they weren't meant to be burdensome. They were designed to show God's people how to live and, most importantly, have a relationship with him. The law, this code of love, was a letter from their heavenly Father designed to foster intimacy between a holy God and sinful mortals.

But as we know, things went awry. Israel rebelled. They broke God's laws. They worshipped other gods. They warred with one another. Repeatedly God sent prophets to warn them to turn from their sin and seek his face. But they ignored these messengers and even killed them. So God judged them with invasions and ultimately exile. After centuries the covenant was in tatters, and the people of God scattered all over the earth.

At this point, you might think the story would be over. God's patience was exhausted. The temple was destroyed. The Israelites were shackled and en route to Babylon. You almost expect God to wash his hands of the whole mess, to decide he'd had enough of his stubborn creation. But he wasn't finished, not by a long shot. Just when we think God's writing a tragedy, it turns out to be a redemptive drama.

He had another plan. "I will make a *new* covenant," he announced through the prophet Jeremiah (Jer. 31:31). "I will put my law in their minds / and write it on their hearts" (v. 33). This new covenant would be something radical. It would internalize the knowledge of God while spreading the message to all humanity. It would produce the kind of intimacy that God wanted with his creation all along. But at that point it was just a prophecy, a vision to be realized through future events. Ultimately, it would be the most costly plan of all. It would demand God do something unthinkable. It would require an act of stubborn, sacrificial love. It would mean writing the new covenant with the blood of his Son.

## KNOWN AND LOVED

The nineteenth-century poet Francis Thompson famously portrayed God as "The Hound of Heaven." The poem of the same name describes the narrator's flight from God.

> *I fled Him, down the arches of the years;*
> *I fled Him, down the labyrinthine ways*
> *Of my own mind; and in the midst of tears.*[4]

Yet the poem continues to describe that God pursues him with "unhurrying chase, / And unperturbed pace."[5]

C. S. Lewis described God's pursuit of him as a young atheist in similar terms. In his autobiography he recalled feeling "the steady, unrelenting approach of Him whom I so earnestly desired not to meet." He finally surrendered, "the most dejected and reluctant convert in all England."[6]

Such stories of divine pursuit, along with the biblical witness, powerfully illustrate God's passionate love for humanity. But it isn't just humanity in general he loves. He loves us individually. God desires intimacy with you, with me. As someone once said, "He loves each of us as if there was only one of us."

We are conflicted creatures. On the one hand, we want to be known. We have a core-deep need to share the essence of who we are with others. On the other hand, we want others to accept us, to love us. So we create facades, highly edited versions of our true selves that others will find acceptable.

Social-media platforms like Facebook and Twitter bring both desires into sharp focus. They bear witness to our deep desire to be known (why else would we spend hours online divulging details about our lives?). We post pictures and comments about everything, from our favorite foods to our most deeply held beliefs. At the same time, it exposes our tendency to erect facades. We often present idealized versions of our lives. We post the pictures in which we look the thinnest, even if they were taken many years ago. We upload images of our meals from fine restaurants, not of the baloney sandwich we had for lunch. The dullness and drudgery of daily life pales compared to the illusion we construct in our online profiles. As one popular post put it, "Lord, please make my life as good as it looks on Facebook."

Why do we engage in this behavior? Because we fear that if we divulge our true selves, others will reject us. We know the truth about ourselves. We're all too aware, as Marguerite Shuster puts it, that "the reservoir of evil in all of us is deeper than we know, and [our] barriers against its eruption are shockingly fragile."[7] If they knew our deepest failings and darkest thoughts, they wouldn't be our friends, much less love us.

Of course we cannot foist illusions about ourselves on God. The Bible tells us that God numbers the very hairs on your head, that he created your inmost being and knit you together in your mother's womb (Luke 12:7; Ps. 139:13). He sees our motivations and innermost desires, every private impulse. He knows every thought and action—from the moment of our conceptions to our final breaths—and loves us anyway.

It's a terrifying realization—and a freeing one. It means we're completely exposed before a holy God, yet he loves us. No sin is too vile, no condition of our hearts beyond his redemption. The one who knows us best loves us most.

What would happen if we were gripped by this truth? How would our lives change if we let it sink into our psyches, our souls? What if we allowed the reality of God's love to penetrate the marrow of our bones?

I think if we truly grasped the power of that truth—that the sovereign Lord of the universe loves us unconditionally—it would change how we think of ourselves and the way we relate to others.

## FINDING FULFILLMENT

Many of us suffer from Conditional Happiness Disorder. Before you Google the term, let me confess something: I made it up. But I believe it describes an ailment that's all too real. Conditional Happiness Disorder is the crippling impulse to habitually measure your worth in relation to external circumstances. "If I could accomplish this or become more like that, then I'd be happy," we tell ourselves. "If I lose twenty pounds . . . or get a promotion . . . or get married . . . or buy a house." If we reach these treasured milestones, we might finally be able to feel good about ourselves and be happy. The problem, of course, is that it's a complete delusion. Even if we're lucky enough to make the goals we set for ourselves, the moment we attain them, a new set of aspirations sparkles on the horizon. Again we tell ourselves, "If I can just accomplish this or that, I'll be happy"—and the cycle starts anew.

A few years ago, I watched a *60 Minutes* interview with the New England Patriots' star quarterback, Tom Brady. To say that Tom Brady has a lot going for him would be an understatement.

115

He's one of the best players in the NFL, has won three Super Bowls, and of course, he's wealthy. On top of that Brady looks like a model. His chiseled features and luxuriant hair have landed him on the cover of *GQ* magazine repeatedly and led *People* to name him one of the sexiest men alive. He's also married to Brazilian supermodel, Gisele Bündchen.

Considering his incredible fame and fortune, what he had to say in the interview was a shock. "There has got to be more than this," he told *60 Minutes* host Steve Kroft. "Why do I have three Super Bowl rings and still think there's something greater out there for me? A lot of people would think, *Man, you've reached your dream. This is it!* Me, I think, *God, there's gotta be more than this.*"

"What's the answer?" Kroft asked him.

"I wish I knew," Brady said. "I wish I knew."[8]

Brady's eyes seemed tired, sad. His voice was desperate. To me it was a poignant example of the inability of any worldly success or human accomplishment to bring about fulfillment. And it was never meant to. We are designed to find our ultimate contentment in the embrace of God's love. "Our hearts are restless," Augustine wrote, "until they find rest in you."[9]

The self-help industry in the United States is a monster. It generates twelve billion dollars in sales each year. We consume scores of books and other materials designed to help us improve ourselves and find love and meaning. But all the literature and seminars and DVDs have little value if they exclude God from the equation. They offer only empty promises and temporary fixes.[10] Brennan Manning wrote, "Genuine self-acceptance is not derived from the power of positive thinking, mind games, or pop psychology. It is an act of faith in the grace of God alone."[11]

We have a desire to be loved, but all human love fails. People betray us. The most faithful die. Only by anchoring our identities in God's unchanging, unconditional love can we find the meaning and contentment we crave.

## RELATING TO OTHERS

Grasping divine love is essential for a healthy relationship with God. But it has wide-ranging implications for our relationships with others too. When we root our sense of identity in God, everything changes. Once our vertical connection is healthy, the horizontal ones tend to thrive.

However, a cruel irony comes into play when we seek validation from others that only God can provide. When we lean too heavily on human relationships, we actually end up sabotaging them. We become clingy, controlling. We find ourselves piling expectations on people they were never meant to bear. It happens with people we meet for the first time. It happens with our friends. It happens in our marriages. Inevitably something gives, and the relationships are ruined. But when we derive our primary sense of identity from God, we're free to enjoy human relationships in the way they were meant to be experienced.

A friend recently told me about how discovering this principle affected his life. As a teenager, he struggled with insecurity. To try to fit in and gain acceptance at school, he sought out the "cool kids" and emulated their actions in an attempt to impress them. A typical adolescent reaction, but he started to realize it was at odds with the Christian faith he professed. A spiritual breakthrough led him to rethink his desire to be liked by his fellow students. "I made a conscious decision," he said. "I was going to live for God's approval, not others'." For him, that meant befriending kids who weren't part of the in-crowd and being kind to everyone. Once he was secure in who he was in God, he was free to relate to the students in his school with authenticity and kindness. And the strangest thing happened. People started to like him more, even the "cool kids." He exuded confidence rather than neediness, and others were drawn to him.

This principle applies beyond the halls of a high school. When we root our sense of identity in God's great love, we're freed up to love others unreservedly. We may even find people drawn to us because of our confidence and emotional security.

Internalizing God's love expands our hearts for others. "We love because he first loved us," is how the disciple John put it (1 John 4:19). The bold commands of the Bible to love our neighbors, and even our enemies, will quickly sap our natural reserves. But when we are flooded with God's love, it overflows into the lives of others.

## TRANSFORMING LOVE

In the foyer of one of the churches I attended growing up hung a copy of the painting *The Lost Sheep*, by Alfred Soord. The painting depicts a shepherd on his knees, leaning precariously over a cliff. With one arm he steadies himself with a staff. With the other, he reaches down to a sheep stranded on a jutting rock below. The work invokes Jesus' parable of the shepherd who leaves the ninety-nine sheep to search for the one that has wandered away (Matt. 18:12–14). It's a strange story. The shepherd's math is off, his actions perplexing. Like any good love story, it's a desperate one, a tale of stubborn, sacrificial love. The shepherd will go to any length to bring his lost sheep safely back to the fold. Every time I read the parable or see the painting, I'm moved. I doubt there's a better image to illustrate God's relentless desire to reconnect with his creation.

Many people are haunted by a deep-seated fear that God doesn't love them. They think they've strayed too far or sinned too much, and they have a sinking feeling that God's given up the chase. That's why it is so important to keep God's tenacious love at the forefront of our hearts and minds, to be reminded that he loves us unconditionally. Remember the story of Hosea. His marriage to a prostitute was a symbol of God's commitment to unfaithful Israel, but it is also an apt image of God's tireless love for each of us—and we need that love desperately.

This love doesn't leave us unchanged. It softens our hearts. We don't stay prostitutes; we become faithful. "Christ's love, while alluring, is one that demands transformation," is how one writer phrased it.[12] The book of Romans warns us from taking advantage of this great love. "Or do you show contempt for the riches of his kindness, forbearance and patience, not realizing that God's kindness is intended to lead you to repentance?" (2:4). I like the way *The Message* translates that same passage: "God is kind, but he's not soft." Indeed, his kindness is simply too great to leave us in our sin.

Our need for God's love isn't always visible. It's not always on the surface. We can bury it with denial, obscure it with busyness, or drown it with entertainment. But it never goes away. In quiet, honest moments we feel a soul sickness, a desire to connect with the source of life, with the only One who knows us fully and loves us unconditionally. Our need for that love is the imperceptible undercurrent that moves our souls toward God. If we fight it, we will flail wildly through life until we wear ourselves out and go under. When we surrender to its pull, we live a life full of meaning, fulfillment, and divine joy.

# NINE
# INTIMATE BEGINNINGS

**THE LECTURE HALL WAS EMPTY. EITHER THIS WAS THE WRONG**
place or I was early. After double-checking the room number, I
slipped into one of the tablet-arm desks, pulled out my laptop, and
waited for the rest of the class to show up.

It was my first day of seminary.

I had no business being there, really. When people asked me
what I was planning to do with a seminary degree, I mumbled
something about wanting to write. Judging from the reactions I
received, this sounded about as plausible to them as my becoming a professional clown. The truth is I had no clear vocational
objective. And given the fact that it had taken me eight years of
popping in and out of college to secure a bachelor's degree, even
I questioned the decision. I did, however, have a deep desire
to learn about God—and a wife kind enough to support my
decision.

I imagined seminary would be a sort of spiritual safari—a pleasure cruise punctuated by exotic theological sightings. Slogging through thick, systematic theology textbooks and memorizing stacks of Greek vocabulary cards quickly erased these romantic notions.

But there were thrilling discoveries along the way. In fact many of them came in that first class, a two-week intensive Gospels course. It was taught by visiting professor Dr. Craig A. Evans, a prominent scholar and regular on CNN and the Discovery Channel. Evans had a knack for bringing the Bible to life. He would act out scenes from Scripture and take us deep into the ancient world, at one point mimicking the chants of Greek soldiers as they marched in phalanx formation.

His insights about the opening passage of John's gospel (the "prolegomena") were particularly powerful. I gained a new appreciation for John's unique approach. Rather than begin by telling us about Jesus' family lineage (like Matthew) or his birth (like Luke), John starts his story at the cosmic level. With rich symbolism and poetic language, John paints the vivid story of Jesus' coming against the dark canvas of history. What emerges is a dazzling vision of God's holy love.

## THE INCARNATION

The most dramatic example of God's immanence is the incarnation, God becoming a human in the person of Jesus. In Jesus, God not only drew near to us but he became one of us. If any event in Scripture captures the staggering paradox of God's transcendence and immanence, this is it. To gain a better appreciation for this momentous event, step into that seminary class with me, and let's walk through the opening passage of John's gospel.

*"In the beginning was the Word . . ." (John 1:1).*

Does this line sound familiar? If so, it's because it echoes another famous biblical passage, Genesis 1:1: *"In the beginning God created the heavens and the earth."*

John retold the creation account, adding fascinating details about the Word's role in creation. Later we learn that it refers to Jesus, though John didn't tell us that yet. So what is the "Word," or the *Logos*, as it appears in the original language? Unfortunately our English translations don't capture the full meaning of the term. The *Logos* had different meanings to Greeks and Jews, and John was likely drawing on both.

In Greek philosophy, the *Logos* was the unifying rational force that held the universe together. It's a difficult concept to explain because there's really no equivalent in modern thought. It might be helpful to think of how we view a fundamental law of physics, like gravity. But the *Logos* was a far bigger concept. Not only did the *Logos* hold the material world together, but it played a key role in its creation. By the time of Jesus, the *Logos* was also understood as a bridge between a transcendent God and the physical world.[1]

From a Jewish perspective, the concept would have brought to mind mentions of God's word in the Old Testament. This is the word by which God called the universe into existence. It was the same word spoken through the prophets. Scripture repeatedly records that "the word of the LORD came to" a certain prophet. The first verse of John's gospel probably wouldn't have offended early Jewish readers, even the ones who didn't accept Jesus as their Messiah. They knew from reading the Scriptures that God had always had his word.

"*. . . and the Word was with God, and the Word was God*" *(John 1:1).*

We know John echoed the creation story of Genesis by starting with the words "In the beginning." But here we see his narrative actually starts *before* the beginning. We learn that before anything was created, God was with the Word.

This description attests to the Word's divine identity (was God) and unity with the Father (was with God). The English "with" is a poor rendering of the Greek. John wrote that the Word was *pros* God. The preposition *pros* means "toward" or "facing."[2] In other words, the Word was not merely with God. Rather, John depicted the Word face-to-face with the Father.

"*The Word became flesh and made his dwelling among us*" *(John 1:14).*

This is the passage's climactic moment. We discover that the Word became human. Some translate this line, "The Word became flesh and *pitched his tent* among us."[3] After dwelling with the Father from before the creation of heaven and earth, the Word became flesh. The word *flesh* is a translation of the Greek word *sarx*. It's not a pretty word. It's gritty and physical. *Strong's Exhaustive Concordance* says *sarx* comes from a word meaning "flesh (as stripped of the skin)."[4] John could have used a gentler word like *soma*, which refers to the body as a whole. But *sarx* denotes the realm of meat and blood and bodily functions. It also encompasses the realm of sinfulness and human frailty.

Scholar Gary M. Burge wrote that the word would have made ancient readers pause in "stunned silence":

John 1:14 contains the risk, the scandal, and the gospel of the Christian faith: The *Logos* became *sarx*. The center of God's life and thought entered the depths of our world and took up its form, its *sarx*, its flesh, in order to be known by us and to save us. . . . No lowliness, no misery, no sinfulness is beyond God's comprehension and reach. He came among us, embraced our world of *sarx* in his Incarnation, and loved us.[5]

To say that the *Logos* (Word) became *sarx* (flesh) would have been shocking indeed. The fact that the eternal Word entered our realm of weakness and sinfulness only heightens the scandal of the incarnation.

*"For the law was given through Moses; grace and truth came through Jesus Christ" (John 1:17).*

In verse 17, John made another daring move. He argued that Jesus is greater than Moses. That might not sound so daring to you or me. But to the Jews of John's day, these were fighting words. It's impossible to overstate how highly they regarded Moses. As liberator, leader, and lawgiver, Moses towered above other biblical figures, even the patriarchs, Abraham, Isaac, and Jacob. Philo, a Jewish philosopher and contemporary of Jesus, called Moses "the mediator and reconciler of the world." The Essenes, a reclusive, ascetic group who likely produced the Dead Sea Scrolls, placed Moses "next to God" and put to death anyone who dared blaspheme his name.[6]

Moses had done something no other mortal had: he had seen God. The famous sighting took place on Mount Sinai after Moses received the Ten Commandments. Moses implored God, "Show me your glory" (Ex. 33:18). The Lord agreed, but with one condition. He told him, "You cannot see my face, for no one may see me and live" (v. 20). God placed Moses in the cleft of a rock and allowed him to glimpse his glory from behind, as his "glory passes by" (v. 22).

From the beginning of his gospel, John contended for the superiority of Jesus. While Moses glimpsed God for a split second from behind, Jesus dwelled face-to-face with the Father throughout eternity. Moses came down the mountain with the law. Jesus came down from heaven with grace and truth. The takeaway is clear: only Jesus possesses perfect intimacy with the Father. Only he can bring heaven to earth and restore our relationship with God.

## INTENDED CHILDREN

That first seminary course was a whirlwind. Lectures in the day, reading at night. Go to bed, and repeat. The course lasted only weeks, but what I learned continues to resonate.

It's been said that the sign of a good poem is not that you will remember it; it's that upon reading it, you know you'll never be the same. It was a little like that for me studying the gospel of John. The grand, poetic description of the incarnate Word opened my eyes to the radical message of divine love at the heart of the Christian story.

I was captivated by the vision of Jesus face-to-face with the Father, dwelling in unbroken communion throughout eternity past. Think of the implications. It means that intimacy preceded creation, that love was burning before the stars were born. And it was out of the overflow of that love—"all things have been created through him and for him" (Col. 1:16)—that the material world sprang into existence. We learn this universe is no accident. It's not the product of blind forces clashing in cold space. Nor are we an accident, for that matter. No, John told us the story behind the story. And we discover the best news imaginable. In the beginning was love.

The warmth of the biblical accounts stands out even more when you encounter other creation narratives. You may have heard about parallels between the Genesis creation account and other ancient creation stories. It is true, for instance, that the Babylonian creation myth (the Enuma Elish) bears similarities to the Genesis account. Yet when you read these stories, what's more striking than the parallels are the differences. Pagan creation stories read like dark soap operas complete with casts of feuding gods. Typically, in a moment of folly or carelessness one of these deities creates humans, who then live in groveling fear before their capricious creators.

By contrast the Bible describes a single supreme God who purposefully creates humans in his own image and then tenaciously pursues a relationship with them. In most creation sagas we are accidents. But in Genesis and John, we are intended children. We have a loving God who looks upon us with paternal affection. It's like the too-good-to-be-true story every orphan longs to hear. Though separated by sin and circumstance, we have a loving, heavenly Father who longs to gather us into his arms.

John also gave me fresh appreciation for the shocking nature of the incarnation. It's easy to forget that in the person of Jesus, God became a human. Not a floating phantom but a real-life human being with blood and bone and muscle. He became *sarx*. God came near. So near we could literally hear him breathe.

The ancient heresy of Docetism (meaning "God with a mask") held that Jesus merely appeared to be human. People couldn't accept the idea of God taking on flesh, so they invented the theory that Jesus' humanity was all an illusion, a divine ruse. Not so. The gospel writers are blunt in depicting Jesus' human qualities. He got hungry. He became angry. He fell asleep in boats. He wept. When led to the cross, his flesh was as vulnerable to the whips and thorns and nails as anyone's. After six hours of torture, he died.

When I was in high school, a pop song topped the charts called "One of Us" by Joan Osborne. The refrain of the chorus was "What if God was one of us?"[7] It's a good question, no matter what you make of the song's theology. According to John, the answer to that question is simple: God *was* one of us. In Jesus, God made the astounding decision to take on human form to be with us in the most tangible, intimate way possible.

## THE ERA OF INTIMACY

Jesus had a special name for God: Dad.

Of course Jesus didn't say Dad. He said Abba, which in Jesus' native tongue was roughly equivalent to our word *Dad* or *Father*. Every so often I see a well-intentioned teacher or blogger claim that *Abba* meant "Daddy" or "Papa." But those terms are too playful to convey the word's original usage. In the first century, Jewish adults would call their fathers Abba to express both affection and respect. As one scholar wrote, the word captures the "warm confidence and the deep reverence that we have for our Father in heaven."[8]

Abba was an intimate word, and Jesus' use of it was ground-breaking. It was a term of endearment for earthly fathers, but Jesus applied it to God, something no one before him had done. Jesus related to God, his Abba, with unprecedented intimacy. And he encouraged his followers to do the same.

This new sense of intimacy was reflected in the way Christians prayed. Some people are surprised to learn that the way ancient Jews and the earliest Christians prayed would have looked very similar to the way Muslims pray today. They prayed on their knees, often with foreheads pressed to the floor. But the early Christians introduced a significant change. They began standing up when they gathered on Sundays. Rather than hide their faces from heaven, they felt it more appropriate to adopt a posture of joy and expectancy on the Lord's Day.[9] In fact, to this day, Eastern Christians still stand and never prostrate themselves on Sundays in honor of the resurrection.

Not only did the Christians stand when they prayed, but some also raised their hands, as Paul had commanded (1 Tim. 2:8). A Christian sarcophagus (a stone coffin) carving found in the catacombs depicts a man with hands lifted in prayer, attesting to the fact that the practice was characteristic of Christian prayer in the third century AD.[10]

## GREAT AND NEAR

"The final goal of every Christian," wrote R. C. Sproul, "is to be allowed to see what was denied to Moses. We want to see Him face-to-face. We want to bask in the radiant glory of His divine countenance."[11]

Jesus saw what was denied to Moses; he dwelled face-to-face with the Father. And through his sacrificial death, he opened a way for us to experience greater intimacy with God. The New Testament writers elaborated on this theme. Paul wrote that since we have been adopted into God's family, "we cry, *'Abba,* Father'" (Rom. 8:15). The writer of Hebrews encouraged us to "approach God's throne of grace with confidence" (4:16).

This doesn't mean the New Testament is solely about God's intimacy. Nor does the Old Testament speak strictly about God's transcendence. The entire Bible speaks of both. All through Scripture we are reminded that God is both great and near.

Even biblical stories that shout God's greatness and glory whisper his nearness and love. Think of Isaiah's terrifying vision of the Lord exalted above the temple. Yes, the spectacle underscored God's glory and grandeur. At the same time, it sent the message that God was powerfully present. The vision marked the initiation of Isaiah's prophetic ministry, a sign that God was still speaking and guiding his people. God's appearance on Mount Sinai is similar. Dangerous though it was, God descended on the mountain to deliver his law to his people. He was with them, even in the wilderness. When the risen Lord appeared to the disciples on the Emmaus Road, he came as a stranger. Only later did the disciples realize he was also their Lord. Only after did they recall how their hearts burned within them as he walked alongside them, speaking to them (Luke 24:32).

And what he told them changed everything. As he explained the significance of his life, death, and resurrection, something shifted. Trembling cowards became fearless ambassadors. They changed, and ultimately, so did human history.

In the next chapter, we will consider some implications of Christ's sacrifice. My prayer is that, like the disciples, we'll find ourselves changing too.

# TEN
# FACE-TO-FACE

**SOME STRANGE THINGS HAPPENED WHEN JESUS DIED.**

As he languished on the cross, the Gospels record that "darkness came over the whole land" (Mark 15:33; Luke 23:44). The darkness descended at noon (John 19:14) and lasted three hours until Jesus' final breath. In the perpetually sunny Middle East, nightfall at noon would have been strange, to say the least.

What did the darkness mean? Perhaps it mirrored the appalling injustice of it all. The Prince of Peace murdered. God naked and nailed to a cross . . . it's as if light itself could not bear to look. In the words of Shakespeare, "The sun, for sorrow, will not show his head."[1]

In addition to this midday darkness, Matthew reports an earthquake: "The earth shook, the rocks split" (27:51). The event sent shock waves through the natural world, upending diurnal rhythms, jostling tectonic plates. The noonday light was extinguished, and the earth rocked violently. Rocks broke, tombs cracked open, and (amazingly) saints came surging back to life. Clearly, this wasn't just another criminal execution.

When the Roman centurion standing guard—maybe even one of those who had mocked Jesus and gambled for his clothes—witnessed the phenomena, he did an about-face. "Surely," he said, "this man was the son of God."[2]

## THE TORN CURTAIN

Matthew, Mark, and Luke all report that during the moment Jesus breathed his last, the curtain of the temple was torn in two from top to bottom (Matt. 27:51; Mark 15:38; Luke 23:45). The curtain of the temple served an important function. It separated the inner sanctuary called the Holy of Holies from the rest of the temple. In Solomon's time the Holy of Holies housed the ark of the covenant (1 Kings 8:6). It was where God dwelled. The thick veil was needed to cordon off this inner sanctum and shield priests from God's overpowering presence. Only the high priest was permitted to enter the Holy of Holies. Even then he entered only once a year, bowed and barefoot, to bring a blood offering on the Day of Atonement.

This curtain sectioning off the Holy of Holies was nothing like the kind you might hang in your house. It was sixty feet long and stretched from floor to ceiling. The Jewish historian Josephus recorded that the veil was four inches thick, and that horses tied to each side could not pull it apart. If horses couldn't rip it apart, human hands wouldn't have a chance. And it was torn from top to bottom, suggesting something supernatural.

It would be hard to exaggerate the significance of the torn

curtain. It meant something fundamental had changed, not just to the décor of a first-century temple, but in the entire way God related to humanity. It meant the barriers between God and us had been removed. The Holy of Holies was, quite literally, unveiled. No more would animal sacrifices be required. No more intricate rituals of purification needed. Priestly mediation was rendered obsolete. Because of Jesus' sacrifice, everyone, from priest to peasant, could be forgiven. All were free to draw near to God.

And if the torn curtain wasn't a clear enough sign, the Jerusalem Talmud (a collection of rabbinic notes) recorded that in AD 30, the year of Jesus' crucifixion, other strange things started taking place in the temple. The priests would awake to find the Western Light (a symbol of God's abiding presence) inexplicably extinguished and the doors of the temple flung open. The eerie incidents brought a sense of foreboding: "O Temple, why do you frighten us?"[3]

It seems God was making it abundantly clear that Jesus' death changed everything. Rather than restrict his presence to a building, God had opened a way whereby everyone could come freely to him.

The writer of Hebrews summed it up:

> But when Christ came as high priest of the good things that are now already here, . . . He did not enter by means of the blood of goats and calves; but he entered the Most Holy Place once for all by his own blood, thus obtaining eternal redemption. (9:11–12)

What a beautiful, daring gesture of love! Jesus entered the Holy of Holies as both high priest and sacrifice so that we could have intimacy with the Father. This intimacy didn't come cheap. It was purchased with divine blood. It required the Son to suffer and the Father to turn his back on the Son, surrendering him to the clutches of death. But nothing short of death would suffice. Only with Christ's dying cry was the temple curtain torn in two. In light of this incredible sacrifice, Hebrews implores us, "Let us then approach God's throne of grace with confidence, so that we may receive mercy and find grace to help us in our time of need" (4:16).

In chapter 9 we saw how the gospel of John portrayed Jesus dwelling face-to-face with the Father before the creation of the world. The torn curtain means we've been invited into that intimacy. Because of what Jesus did, we can now stand face-to-face with the Father and share in that ancient intimacy. As the apostle Paul wrote, our true lives are "now hidden with Christ in God" (Col. 3:3).

Of course, this restoration of intimacy was what God had in mind all along. "Even before he made the world, God loved us and chose us in Christ," we're told in Ephesians 1:4 (NLT). The psalmist wrote, "For you created my inmost being; / you knit me together in my mother's womb. . . . Your eyes saw my unformed body" (Ps. 139:13, 16). This intimacy fulfills a deep-seated desire in each of us to be known and treasured. I love the way pastor Jonathan Martin put it:

> We were conceived in delight and baptized into wonder before we even had a name. There was one who beheld us in our unformed substance, singing over us, delighting in us. Because the enchantment of divine love was there before we were born, it is native to us; we all have a primal desire inside

of us to be the object of that delight, to be fully known before a God who celebrates us.[4]

## TEMPLES OF FLESH

The Bible calls our bodies "the temple of the living God" (2 Cor. 6:16). If such a statement seems normal, it's only due to familiarity. The first Jews to read that probably fell off their chairs. To them, the temple was everything. And it's not difficult to see why. It held a central place in their Scriptures and, by the time of Jesus, the Jewish temple was a marvel unparalleled in the ancient world. The Talmud boasts, "He who has not seen the Temple of Herod has never seen a beautiful building."[5] The temple and the plaza surrounding it took King Herod decades to complete, even with more than ten thousand workers and all the resources of Rome at his disposal. Herod leveled the top of a mountain, erected retaining walls twenty stories high, and built the temple atop the already impressive foundation. The temple was adorned with so much gold, it was said to look directly at it in the daylight was to risk going blind.

The extravagance was appropriate for a site of such weighty theological significance. Jerusalem was the heart of the Jewish cosmos, and the temple was the heart of Jerusalem. Most important, it was the very dwelling place of the Lord Almighty. But Jesus spoke of a change. "A time is coming when you will worship the Father neither on this mountain nor in Jerusalem. . . . The true worshipers will worship the Father in the Spirit and in truth" (John 4:21, 23). The locus of God's presence was shifting, from a structure made of stone to ones made of flesh. It's an astonishing move. God exchanged the temple's grandeur for the fragile human frame. The Creator of the universe decided to take up residence in these humble dwellings of bones and blood. It's almost beyond comprehension, yet that's what the Bible says. Your body, my body—God's temple.

The Jewish temple really had one function. Behind all the detailed ordinances and intricate craftsmanship for the temple's construction, beneath the tedious priestly procedures was this purpose: to be a dwelling place for God.

Could it be that our purpose, our function is exactly the same? To serve as God's dwelling place?

It sounds grandiose, I know. The dwelling place of the Lord Almighty. Imagine what we'd think of someone who listed that on his or her résumé. At the same time it seems too simple. Most of us would prefer to be handed a spiritual to-do list. If I can maximize my good deeds and minimize my sins, then I'll be okay with God. It might be hard, but at least it's tangible. There's no ambiguity. With enough grit and determination, I can get there. I can *do* something. But being a dwelling place is a passive enterprise. It means simply welcoming God into your life, that you're a vessel for his presence. Yet that's also what makes it so freeing. It secures your identity. Being God's dwelling place means your worth isn't tied up in what people think about you. Instead of scrambling to collect achievements and accolades, you're able to rest in the fact that you're a temple. And a temple doesn't have to do anything; a temple just is.

You're never going to be perfect, but you don't have to be. A temple that's a little broken down or faded on the outside is still a temple, if God's presence is there. His presence in you is what matters most. Just be sure the curtain is down, that there is nothing partitioning God's presence from other parts of your life. Remember, the torn curtain in the temple didn't erase God's holiness; it let his holiness out. He wants to do the same thing in your life. He desires to remove whatever comes between you and him. He longs to dwell in you and make your whole life holy.

## SWIMMING IN LOVE

The message of the torn curtain is a powerful one. It's a testament to God's white-hot love for us. But it's all too possible to understand God's love, yet not experience it. We can contemplate the cross, hear Christ's final cry of anguish, see the temple curtain torn, and walk away unchanged. The gospel requires mental assent; we must believe and confess it. Knowledge of God's love is essential, but not adequate. It must be experienced too.

To illustrate the point, let me ask you a question. Would you rather . . .

a. swim Australia's Great Barrier Reef?
b. read about it on Wikipedia?

Before you answer, I think you should know there's a compelling case to be made for option B. Mere minutes on Wikipedia will teach you more about the Great Barrier Reef than you could learn in weeks of physical exploration. Sure, snorkel and scuba dive the reef, and you'll be dazzled by subaquatic beauty. But you won't learn that you're swimming the largest coral reef system on the planet, the only structure created by living organisms that's visible from space. Nor would you discover that the natural wonder has more than nine hundred individual reefs and nine hundred islands, stretching for sixteen hundred miles over an area of 133,000 square miles. You'd be oblivious to the fact that the Reef is home to thirty species of whales, dolphins, and porpoises, and more than fifteen hundred species of fish. If you were prepping for an exam about the Reef, choosing to read Wikipedia would be a far wiser investment of your time.

Not convinced? Yeah, me neither. I'd go with option A. And unless you have some sort of aversion to ocean adventures, I'm guessing you would too. I've never visited the Great Barrier Reef, but I'm certain no number of factoids, regardless of how interesting, could replace the experience of slicing through the blue-green waters or watching schools of tropical fish flash through its intricate, spiny structures. Knowing about the Reef could never compare to experiencing it.

It's the same with God's love. Simply knowing about God can never take the place of experiencing him. You could gather facts about God for the rest of your life and he could still be a virtual stranger to you. You can observe the flame but never be warmed by the fire. Late in life the great theologian and philosopher Thomas Aquinas had a powerful encounter with God. Afterward, he stopped writing abruptly. When pressed for an explanation, he responded, "Everything I have written seems like straw by comparison with what I have seen and what has been revealed to me."[6] Even to this genius, who produced such foundational works as the *Summa Theologica*, knowing about God was not the same as experiencing him.

That's not to belittle the importance of learning about God. Knowledge is crucial. Without reading up on the Great Barrier Reef, for example, you might not even know it exists, much less have a desire to visit it. Researching its marvels whets your appetite to explore it. Then there's all the information you need to get there (itinerary, tickets, maps), not to mention the complex aeronautical engineering you must rely on just to get to Australia.

In the same way, knowledge of God is critical. J. I. Packer said theology (the study of God) helps us "appreciate the greatness, goodness, and glory of God."[7]

But unless we experience God, we don't truly know him. Nowhere is this truer than when it comes to God's love. Acknowledging his love is one thing. Letting it penetrate your heart and living in light of its reality is another thing altogether.

## ADOPTED CHILDREN

My wife and I have friends who recently adopted two children from Ghana. After months of paperwork and two trips to Africa, they came home with a four-year-old girl and her six-year-old brother.

Excited as the adoptive parents were, the transition wasn't easy. They had the challenge of assimilating the adopted children with their three biological kids. But the biggest challenges stemmed from behaviors the adopted children had acquired in their first years of life. Before being taken in by an orphanage, they lived on the streets. Their short lives had been marked by scarcity and neglect.

As the adopted children settled into their new home, the deprivation manifested itself in puzzling behaviors. Initially, they found sharing nearly impossible. Just the sight of another child playing with a toy they wanted was enough to set off a forty-minute crying fit. Once they finished playing with a toy, they would sometimes break it to ensure no other child could play with it. At mealtimes, they would gorge themselves. If they saw the cereal or milk running low, they got nervous. "Is there plenty, Mommy and Daddy? Is there plenty?" they would ask. Despite their parents' assurances, they drank milk till they were sick. At one point, their parents took them to the grocery store and pointed out the rows of refrigerated milk. "See, there is so much milk. We will never run out."

Despite these challenges, they are seeing progress. The children are beginning to bond with their new parents and siblings. They are learning the rules of the house. Slowly they are gaining confidence that they are loved, that they have a family, and that their needs will always be met.

I think we're a lot like those children.

We've all picked up bad habits along the way—and it's not hard to see why. We've been raised on the streets. By the streets I mean this world. It's a place where only the strong survive, where you have to scratch and claw for everything you get. The powerful, talented, beautiful, and wealthy are rewarded. The weak are crushed. It's a reality reinforced in every arena and stage of life: on the playground, at school, in sports, in dating, in social circles, in the job market. So we jockey for position and angle for opportunities and look out for number one. We know life's not a zero-sum game. For every success someone else has, one disappears for us. So we learn to build ourselves up and knock others down. We're conditioned by a system engineered to foster fear and selfishness. We become survivors.

Then one day something miraculous happens. God adopts us. We join his family. Suddenly we find ourselves loved, cherished.

We're introduced to a whole new way of living, one in which the last are first, the meek are blessed, and we love rather than hate our enemies.

But old habits die hard, and we find ourselves reverting to old ways. We doubt God's love. We cast sideways glances at our dwindling resources. We drink all the milk. We wonder if God will really provide for us. Not just possessions but meaning, pleasure, and most of all, love.

I'm convinced that there's really one big question at the heart of life and that our answer to this question will ripple throughout our time on earth and into eternity. The question is simply this: *are you going to believe that God loves you?*

The Bible says again and again that you can. It says that God has loved you with an everlasting love, that at his right hand are pleasures forevermore, that he owns the cattle on a thousand hills, that he goes to prepare a place for you, that he's coming back to get you.

There will always be plenty for you. Not the spoils of the street, but the treasures of your Father. You can trust him. Rest in him. Breathe.

He's always loved you. And he always will.

# ELEVEN
# JESUS IN THE SHADOWS

**IN JESUS, GOD CAME TO EARTH. THE DIVINE WORD, PRESENT** from before creation, "came down from heaven . . . and was made man," as the Nicene Creed puts it. This truth is foundational to our faith. We celebrate it at Christmas, proclaim it in the church, and acknowledge it when we pray.

We've looked at how this momentous event opened up a new intimacy with the Almighty. But it has another astonishing implication: it means that God understands what it's like to be human. He has literally been in our shoes, our skin. As a result he knows what it's like to be hungry, to feel pain, to be rejected, to suffer loss, even to die.

A suffering Messiah has always been difficult for people to accept. Paul wrote that the idea of a crucified Messiah was a "stumbling block" to the Jews and "foolishness" to the Greeks (1 Cor. 1:23). Even today it presents evangelistic challenges.

Muslims, for instance, accept Jesus' virgin birth and anticipate his second coming, yet deny the crucifixion. It was a different man on the cross, they say, one who merely looked like Jesus. Though Christians don't deny the crucifixion, we still have a tendency to tame Christ's suffering. A suffering Messiah has a way of making us uncomfortable, especially if we enjoy lives of relative ease and affluence. Unfortunately, when we give in to this temptation, we end up taming God. The majesty of God cannot be separated from the suffering of his Son. As James Stewart wrote, "Behind Calvary is the throne of heaven."[1] To discount Christ's suffering is to diminish God's glory.

Ultimately we need a suffering Messiah. Regardless of where we live or how much we have, pain and loss will eventually invade our lives. The incarnation means God is with us in our pain. He not only came to earth, but he suffered. And when we suffer, he knows exactly how we feel.

## FELLOW SUFFERER

I gained a whole new appreciation for Christ's suffering when I traveled to Albania in the summer of 1999 for a short-term relief mission.

I arrived right at the end of the Kosovo War. NATO bombings had finally forced Slobodan Milosevic, the "Butcher of the Balkans," to halt his genocidal campaign against the ethnic Albanians of his country. But thousands of refugees were still flooding into Albania from Kosovo every day.

There was no time to settle in. On our first morning there, the director of the orphanage where I was staying took me and several other volunteers down to the refugee receiving center. This was where I would spend the majority of my time, unpacking trucks of aid arriving from Europe and distributing the food and supplies to refugees.

I was twenty years old, a pastor's kid from the prairies of Alberta, Canada. Nothing I'd ever experienced prepared me for what I was about to encounter. Every day refugees arrived by the busload. They would spend a couple of weeks in the receiving center before being relocated to a refugee camp. Life at the camps was tough, but conditions at the receiving center were far worse.

The receiving center, a small sports complex with a high-school-sized gymnasium, became a temporary home to as many as fifteen hundred refugees at a time during the crisis. At night bodies blanketed the gym floor and the small set of bleachers. The complex had only two primitive bathrooms. The toilets were constantly backing up and flooding the hallway leading to the gym. Going outside for fresh air meant wading through an inch or so of human waste. Many of the refugees had traveled for days, and showers were not available. The smell in the complex was almost unbearable. Yet the refugees didn't complain. They were so numb they hardly seemed to notice.

A week earlier I had stood in front of my church at home to explain the mission. A friend and I were going to Albania, I told the congregation, to help the Albanian refugees flooding into the country from Kosovo. I was optimistic, excited even. My desire to go was fuelled by a sense of adventure as much as anything else, and I had lofty expectations. I pictured myself filing through a crowd of refugees like Mother Teresa, feeding and comforting people. I would be an instrument of God's peace.

My naive hopes crashed hard. I hadn't anticipated what it was like to encounter raw grief, and when I did, my instinctive response was to avert my eyes, not rush toward it. I was actually grateful for the never-ending strenuous and mundane duties. Carrying food, distributing medicine, even cleaning bathrooms was better than having to look into the eyes of these people who had lost so much. I was thankful, too, for the language barrier. If I did speak their language, what could I say? How could I even begin to comfort people who had lost everything? Any encouragement would be inadequate. In the shadow of death, words of comfort can sound hollow. I remember watching one young Albanian lady who had just seen her husband murdered trying her best to nod politely as the words of a counselor died in midair.

When we had a translator present, we listened to their stories. I had heard of the horrors of ethnic cleansing on the news, but that's nothing like sitting face-to-face with the people afflicted. Many had witnessed members of their families murdered. Others had been separated from their families and didn't even know if they were alive. Many had watched their houses burned before being forced to run for their lives. Even once the violence was over, most would have nothing for which to return. As they told their stories, I sat and listened, my eyes focused on the ground and filling with tears—quite different from the heroic role I had envisioned for myself.

Every night I left the receiving center and returned to the relative safety of the orphanage, but I was finding it difficult to leave the stories I had heard behind. As I lay in bed, they replayed in my mind. The contrast from my comfortable life at home to this reality was sharp. I had grown up with all my needs fulfilled. The people I loved were safe.

My faith was also under fire. For me, the tenets of the Bible had always been easy to accept. I readily believed in God's love. After all, I had always felt loved by my family and friends. I embraced the fact that good would ultimately triumph over evil. It made sense. The good things in my life always seemed to outnumber the bad.

Where was God for these people? What relevance did Christianity have for a refugee? As I grasped for the roots of my faith, I found that even the most profound theology and inspirational ideas I heard in church had a strange way of sounding empty in this part of the world.

About the time I was wrestling with these thoughts, another volunteer approached me with an idea. He wanted to give the refugees a one-page summary of the Bible as we distributed aid. Before he had it translated he asked me to read it. It was a very basic synopsis of the Bible. At first I wasn't too keen about any sort of evangelistic attempts under such conditions, let alone an effort to summarize the entire Bible on one page of paper. But I kept an open mind and tried to imagine how it would look through the eyes of a refugee.

The summary whistled through the Old Testament, introduced Jesus, and briefly described his life. Then came the story of the crucifixion.

"Jesus was tortured and killed by men."

The sentence jolted me. Of course I knew the story of the Gospels well, but I felt like I was reading this part for the first time. In the context of my surroundings I saw Jesus in a whole new way. His suffering seemed more real than ever before. I saw him alone and afraid. I saw him as one who knew what it meant to lose everything, in a strange land, as a refugee.

149

# A PERSON, NOT ANSWERS

The Bible offers no escape from the problem of suffering. And no easy answers for the pain we experience in this world.

Don't get me wrong—it has plenty to say on the subject. It tells us that suffering builds character, turns us to God, and even brings redemption. But ultimately Scripture presents no philosophical formula explaining why we suffer. Even the book of Job, a veritable suffering saga, is silent on the topic. Job's friends offer their beleaguered buddy various explanations, but they're all wrong. And when God finally shows up, it's not to answer questions.

This can be frustrating, especially for those of us drawn to life's big questions. We want to know *why*. Yet for people in the throes of suffering, the Bible offers something much different than an answer—it offers a Person.

The Bible tells us we're not alone, no matter how deep our suffering. The writer of Hebrews described Jesus as our High Priest who can "empathize with our weaknesses" (4:15). This is crucial. Identifying with someone's pain requires that you have at least some experience of his or her suffering. The word *compassion* comes from the Latin *compassio*, which literally means "to suffer with."[2] Only one willing to suffer truly has compassion. That's why German theologian Jürgen Moltmann insisted that all theology must be conducted "within earshot of the dying Christ."[3]

On his 39th birthday, poet Christian Wiman was diagnosed with an incurable form of blood cancer. He wrote frankly about the agonizing effects of his illness and the treatments.

> I have had bones die and bowels fail; joints lock in my face and
> arms and legs, so that I could not eat, could not walk . . . I have

passed through pain I could never have imagined, pain that seemed to incinerate all my thoughts of God and to leave me sitting there in the ashes, alone.[4]

When the diagnosis came, Wiman was a rising star in the literary world and editor of *Poetry*, the world's most prestigious poetry publication. Though Wiman confessed his Christian faith had "evaporated in the blast of modernism and secularism to which I was exposed in college," the diagnosis started a journey that ultimately led him back to God. It wasn't a particular doctrine that drew him back to the faith. Even the resurrection, he admits, was a struggle for him to accept. But Wiman found a friend in the suffering Messiah.

> I am a Christian because of that moment on the cross when Jesus, drinking the very dregs of human bitterness, cries out, *My God, my God, why has thou forsaken me*. . . . The point is that God is *with us*, not beyond us, in suffering. I am a Christian because I understand that moment of Christ's passion to have meaning in my own life, and what it means is that the absolute solitary and singular nature of extreme human pain is an illusion. I'm not suggesting that ministering angels are going to come down and comfort you as you die. I'm suggesting that Christ's suffering shatters the iron walls around individual human suffering.[5]

In the face of brutal, isolating pain there is no substitute for the presence of Christ. I have never experienced anything like Wiman's pain, yet I, too, find myself drawn to Christ's suffering. Jesus' struggle in the Garden of Gethsemane always moves me.

Both Matthew and Mark recorded that before his crucifixion, Jesus was "deeply distressed and troubled" and "overwhelmed with sorrow to the point of death" (Mark 14:33; Matt. 26:38). Withdrawing from his disciples, he began to pray. And it was a desperate prayer, a prayer of agony. Falling on his face he cried, "Abba, Father. . . . Take this cup from me" (Mark 14:36). Luke added that as he prayed, "his sweat was like drops of blood falling to the ground" (22:44). Religion professor Johnnie Moore offered this insight into the way we should envision Jesus:

> When you picture him, you shouldn't picture him with a halo on his head. You should picture him with dirty feet on the way to a leper colony or sweat rolling down his brow from turning the temple's tables over. And, you should picture him weeping so uncontrollably that his tears become blood when he envisions the weight of the world's wrong landing squarely on his shoulders.[6]

We can only guess as to exactly what was going on in Jesus' heart when he was in Gethsemane. He knew what was coming, so he was certainly anticipating torture and death. But there was also a spiritual blackness: the silence of his Father, the sins of the world. It's a dreadful scene, one made even more awful by the fact that the cup was not taken from him. In obedience, he went to the cross and died a criminal's death. If there was ever anyone who knew suffering, it was Jesus.

Many of his followers have known it too. And in their pain, they have experienced the comfort of the Man of Sorrows beside them. The late Romanian minister Richard Wurmbrand spent fourteen years in Communist prisons. During his imprisonments he was tortured repeatedly and spent three years in solitary confinement. He gave this account of what comforted him during those dark years:

> I've told the West how Christians were tied to crosses for four days and four nights. The crosses were put on the floor and other prisoners were tortured and made to fulfill their bodily necessities upon the faces and the bodies of the crucified ones. I have since been asked, 'Which Bible verse helped and strengthened you in those circumstances?' My answer is, 'No Bible verse was of any help.' Bible verses alone are not meant to help. We knew Psalm 23. But when you pass through suffering you realize that it was never meant by God that Psalm 23 should strengthen you. It is the Lord who can strengthen you, not the psalm that speaks of Him doing so. It is not enough to have the psalm. You must have the One about whom the psalm speaks.[7]

Wurmbrand had the highest respect for the Bible. He risked his life and freedom to smuggle Bibles into Communist countries during the Cold War. But he understood that in the face of death and suffering, only the presence of the living Christ could bring true comfort and strength.

You probably haven't been imprisoned or tortured, but we all know what it's like to suffer. Maybe it's the death of a family member, a shattered family, a broken friendship, or a chronic health issue. Whatever the source of your pain, you are not alone. You have a divine companion who knows what you're going through. And in the end, I think that's what we all really need. Not just an answer to why we suffer. Not mere intellectual satisfaction about why evil befalls us. We need someone to suffer with us, a Savior whose cross stands beside the losses of our lives.

## CROSS COMFORT

Before traveling to Albania, I read the account of the crucifixion very differently. When Jesus wept in Gethsemane, I simply saw it as a test. His anguished cry from the cross was a prelude to triumph. Most sermons I heard emphasized the victorious moments of the crucifixion. Pastors thundered Jesus' final words from the pulpit, "It is finished!" Yet Jesus' cry of doubt and despair seemed always to be read in hushed tones, like we were all a little embarrassed by Jesus' loneliness, by his vulnerability. It was unpleasant to encounter such raw emotion in the manicured world of the West. In multimillion-dollar sanctuaries to people in dresses or fifty-dollar cargo shorts, the cry of this suffering, first-century Messiah seemed strange indeed.

Ajith Fernando, a Christian leader from Sri Lanka who ministers to the urban poor, wondered if Western Christians have discounted this crucial aspect of the gospel. He wrote:

> I think one of the most serious theological blind spots in the western church is a defective understanding of suffering. There seems to be a lot of reflection on how to avoid suffering and on what to do when we hurt. We have a lot of teaching about escape from suffering and therapy for suffering, but there is inadequate teaching about the theology of suffering.[8]

The picture of the suffering God is not a popular one. In our affluent societies, it has a way of getting crowded out.

But in Albania, Jesus' pain was welcomed. As I looked at the faces of those whose lives had been shattered by tragedy, I heard his cry anew, in all the rich depth of his agony. "My God!" he cried from the cross. "Why did you leave me?" It's possible the cry in their hearts was much the same.

Prior to being in Albania, I always rushed through the gospel narrative, eager for the resolution of resurrection morning. But I had missed the equally important message of that dark day of crucifixion. I was now able to freeze Jesus in his moment of anguish and resist the urge to fast-forward.

His pain was important. It was the point at which God's world intersected with ours. It was God displaying his love with sheer abandon and letting us know that no matter what happens, we'd never be alone. Even in the darkest night our fingers would find the steady beam of his suffering, and the pierced hands of his love.

## *JEZUS* SAVES

One day we took a break from our relief work to accompany a group of Christian youth on a picnic. For these young Albanians the future was bleak. Mafia gangs were powerful in the country, influencing every level of government. Albania offered little for young people not willing to join organized crime, and the dictatorial government's policies made leaving the country almost impossible. Though Albania had been freed from the grip of its

Communist government in 1990, the atheistic sentiment in the nation was still strong, and Christians were routinely persecuted.

At the picnic, there was a time of sharing. One teen jumped up to give his testimony, pulling up his shirt to reveal the scars from two gunshot wounds. He had been shot on account of his newfound faith. Though he had nearly died, his spirit had not been dampened. In fact the whole group surged with the same electric joy. Fearlessly they were reaching out to their friends, telling them about their love for Jesus.

The next Sunday I went to church with them. The small church service was held in a dilapidated building buzzing with flies. Outside, packs of wild dogs barked incessantly. Added to these distractions was the ubiquitous threat of danger. In this fledgling church, pastors were appointed on the basis of spiritual seniority.

"He's the oldest Christian in the congregation," our translator whispered to me as a young man walked up front to give the sermon. "He's twenty-two."

I didn't speak the language, but the songs sung during the worship time had familiar tunes. From listening to them, I had learned enough to understand the name of Jesus in Shqip, the native language of Albania: *Jezus.* Although I understood little of the message, I noticed each time Jesus' name was mentioned.

Rhythmic as waves, the name would come in the sermon, spoken with more and more feeling each time. The young pastor did not have the forceful style of many Western preachers. He spoke softly, and his demeanor was calm. Instead of pointing aggressively or chopping the air for emphasis, his hands remained folded neatly behind his back. He stood before the small congregation wearing shorts and a T-shirt. He had no pulpit. As he

talked his eyes brimmed with tears. Finally, on the verge of crying, he tripped over the name: "Je-zus," he said, wiping his eyes.
For a while he stood in silence. Then he smiled broadly as tears
ran down his cheeks. He looked out across the congregation.

"Jezus," he said again.

# TWELVE
# THE FRAGRANCE OF ETERNITY

**A COUPLE OF YEARS AGO I ATTENDED THE GLOBAL LEADERSHIP**
Summit, a conference for church and business leaders. The
Summit is held each year at Willow Creek Community Church
and draws approximately seven thousand people with one hun-
dred thousand more watching live at locations all over the world.
Past speakers include Colin Powell, Condoleezza Rice, Jimmy
Carter, Tony Blair, Tony Dungy, Jack Welch, Andy Stanley, and
Rick Warren.

I was there for work. As an editor of a publication for pastors, I knew there would be interesting content for our readers.
As I scanned the lineup for that year, one speaker seemed out
of place. She wasn't a prominent politician or business tycoon or
megachurch pastor. Rather than wearing a suit, she wore a long
white robe with a headscarf. She was known as "Mama Maggie,"
a diminutive Coptic Christian who worked in the slums of Cairo,

Egypt. When Bill Hybels, pastor of Willow Creek and founder of the conference, introduced her, he seemed uneasy.

"Mama Maggie doesn't fit the conventional understanding of success," he said. "I'll confess, at first I didn't think she was right for the Summit . . . but I've come around."

As he worked his way through the introduction, it was clear others had pushed to include her and he had reluctantly agreed. Regardless, when Mama Maggie walked onstage, the crowd erupted. She was visibly moved by the reaction. Stopping midway to the podium, she pressed her hands together and looked up, mouthing words that were lost amid the thunderous applause. Then she lowered her body to the floor and prayed for a moment before rising to speak.

She was worth applauding. Mama Maggie has dedicated her life to feeding and educating homeless, starving children in Manshiyat Naser (or "Garbage City," as it's known to most people in Egypt). She founded an organization called Stephen's Children to help the thousands of children who roam the trash heaps looking for scraps of food. Today the organization has seven hundred staff and fifteen hundred volunteers, many of whom were helped by the charity as children.

Most of the conference's sessions focused on success strategies and principles of organizational leadership. Mama Maggie, however, aimed her talk at the level of the soul. First she spoke of the children.

"When I touch a poor child, I touch Jesus Christ. When I listen to a poor child, I'm listening to God's heart beating for all humanity."

Then she shared some leadership insights, but they were spiritual, mystical, nothing like those offered by the other speakers.

Silence is the secret. Silence your heart to listen to your spirit. Silence your spirit to listen to His Spirit. In silence you leave many and be with the One. The hardest task of a leader is to get to know the Almighty and to keep your heart pure.[1]

That evening, after the sessions, a colleague and I had the opportunity to interview her. As we waited for her in a window-less room in the bowels of the church, we weren't quite sure what to expect. I had interviewed scores of ministry leaders, but she was different. What do you ask a living saint and modern-day mystic?

When she arrived, she immediately put us at ease. Scrounging through a bag, she produced handfuls of candies, which she dis-tributed to each person in the room. *She's so used to being around kids*, I remember thinking, *she treats adults like children*. Or maybe she knew that deep down the two aren't all that different. She also gave us each a miniature wooden cross, carved by the chil-dren in Egypt.

Still her faith seemed so ethereal, otherworldly. We strug-gled to know where to start.

We asked about the frequent comparisons people have made between her and Mother Teresa. She smiled and shook her head slowly. "I am not worthy to untie her sandal," she said, "but we have the same Lover."

Had she'd ever experienced a "dark night of the soul," a time when she struggled with a feeling of God's absence?

"In the fire you are either burned or become pure. God's love is fire. It consumes or purifies. Everyone who carries the fragrance of eternity has to experience the dark valley of death."

The profound, penetrating responses barely registered above

a whisper. But more impressive than anything she said was her presence. There was almost a palpable humility about her, an incredible gentleness of spirit.

For days I couldn't stop thinking about meeting Mama Maggie. What made her witness so powerful?

It wasn't solely what she said, or even what she did, commendable though it was. It was the combination of the two. She was a mystic, in the best sense of the word. Her mind was on things above, and she had an acute sense of spiritual reality. At the same time, she was immersed in the greatest needs of humanity. She hadn't holed up in some commune to meditate on spiritual truths; she spent her days and nights with the unloved and forgotten. She was at once otherworldly and down-to-earth. "Some people are too heavenly minded to be of any earthly good," the old expression goes. Well, not Mama Maggie. She was definitely heavenly minded, but it only served to make her of more earthly good. Her spirit was in the heavens, but her hands were on the ground.

I think it's that combination, that paradox, which made her so compelling. In her life I glimpsed a reflection of the dual nature of God's otherness and love.

## CHRIST AND CULTURE

If you've made it this far, you know this book is first and foremost about God. That is by design. I believe that if we build our theology from the bottom up, starting with humanity, we're almost sure to get God wrong. Inevitably we project our biases and wishes heavenward and end up with a god who looks suspiciously familiar, a god made in our own image. We end up bowing before the mirror.

Things turn out a lot better if we start at the other end of the spectrum and proceed in the opposite direction. When we build our theology from the top down—that is, beginning with God— we gain a more accurate view of God and ourselves as well. Only then can we hope to see ourselves in the light of divine reality. As Teresa of Avila said, "We shall never succeed in knowing ourselves unless we seek to know God."[2]

We've seen God as transcendent and immanent, holy and loving, other and intimate. We considered what these twin attributes mean for our relationship with God and for our identity. I want to conclude by moving in a slightly different direction. Let's explore what God's otherness and intimacy mean for how we relate to the rest of the world.

Too often we answer the question by looking around instead of up. We take our cues from ministry models that succeed in attracting lots of people. Even weighing biblical passages that stress purity against ones about love can miss the point. What we need to do is look at God. I'm convinced his very nature holds the secret. The divine otherness and intimacy provides the model for how we can relate to outsiders with both conviction and love.

The relationship between Christians and the surrounding culture is a topic of endless debate. A variety of models have been suggested.

Some call for isolation. *The world is evil! We must withdraw to maintain our purity. Listen to Christian music. Read only Christian books. Stay away from theaters. Pull your kids out of public school.* You get the idea.

The other extreme is full immersion. *Adopt the ways of the world. Consume all the same entertainment. Participate in the same activities. Support the same causes. The goal isn't to avoid the world; it's to become indistinguishable from it. When we affirm the beliefs and behaviors of outsiders, they will feel loved and accepted by us.*

Most of us fall somewhere in between these two extremes. We don't have an isolationist mentality. Retreating to a Christian bubble is not only impractical; it's unscriptural. We're called to love our neighbors, not run from them. On the other hand, we have serious reservations about the dominant values of mainstream culture. We realize there must be something different about us if we claim to follow Christ.

So how can we love people while retaining our Christian identity?

## PECULIAR CHILDREN

One of the most common metaphors employed in Scripture is a familial one. God is our Father. We are his children. Children don't look exactly like their parents, but they certainly bear a resemblance. It's the same with God and us. The writer of Ephesians told us to "be imitators of God as dear children" (5:1 NKJV).

But how do we imitate God's otherness? Unlike him, we do not transcend the material world. We are not superior to the rest of humanity. But as his children, we should possess a quality of otherness. We belong to a kingdom Jesus said was "not of this world (John 18:36)," and the Bible repeatedly stresses this unique identity. "Our citizenship is in heaven" (Phil. 3:20). We are described as "foreigners and exiles . . . a chosen people, a royal priesthood, a holy nation, God's special possession" (1 Pet. 2:11, 9). I prefer the way the last part of verse 9 reads in the King James: "You are . . . a peculiar people." It's an echo of Exodus 19:5, where the Lord calls Israel his "peculiar treasure."

Peculiar isn't the most flattering adjective. We often use it euphemistically, maybe as a polite way of saying that someone is eccentric or a little off. Peculiar people stand out. They may violate social norms and make others uncomfortable. They behave differently.

We're not called to be socially awkward or maladjusted, but we should stand out. We should be peculiar. The fruit of the Spirit—love, joy, peace, forbearance, kindness, goodness, faithfulness, gentleness, and self-control (Gal. 5:22–23)—should be visible in our lives. Of course we'll never achieve perfection. We can't lapse into legalism or rely on good deeds to earn God's favor. But by the power of the Spirit, we should strive to embody the values of the kingdom. And those values will strike people as strange.

I remember one of the first theology lessons I ever received. The professor was my mom. I was about ten years old when she sat me down to explain what she called God's "upside-down kingdom."

"To God, everything is backwards and upside-down," she told me. "The first are last, the strong are weak, and the rich are poor."

At the time, her words didn't make a lot of sense, but she was on to something. There does seem to be an inverted logic to life in the kingdom, and the Bible teaches us to embrace these "upside-down" values. That means loving the unlovely, befriending the outcasts, and celebrating the people the world disregards. G. K. Chesterton defined a saint as "one who exaggerates what the world neglects." The same should be true of all Christians.

I've heard the church described as a colony of God's kingdom on earth. I like that. It captures the otherness, the distinctiveness of our identity. It communicates that this is not our home. We're ambassadors. Right now we look weak, but it's only because we live in occupied territory. The church is a small outpost of a mighty kingdom. And the King is coming.

## BEYOND TRUTH GRENADES

Maintaining our distinctiveness is crucial. Yet we can't fortify ourselves inside the colony and lose contact with the outside world. Our otherness must be balanced with love.

I read about an attention-grabbing object lesson a pastor named Ken Korver used in one of his sermons. He took a paper bag filled with balls into the pulpit with him. In the middle of his sermon, he knelt down behind the pulpit, and pretended to defend himself against "the outside world" as if the pulpit was a shield. As he hid behind the pulpit, he started hurling the balls—"truth bombs," as he called them—into the congregation.[3]

As he bombarded his parishioners, he unpacked the lesson: God does not intend for us to hurl disembodied truths at people. Then he challenged the audience to consider what God did in the incarnation: instead of merely hurling truth bombs, God sent his Son to walk among us, communicating truth up close and personally.

It's a good lesson. A lot of us are far more comfortable lobbing rhetorical grenades at the surrounding culture from the safety of our holy huddle than actually going out and loving people.

True love, of course, never happens from a distance. Love is a tangly thing. It involves being willing to suffer. In Jesus, God did just that. He bridged the yawning chasm between heaven and earth and came down to rescue and redeem us. As his children, we have to be willing to take great pains to reach others and love them.

I have to confess this is tough for me. It's not that I fear contamination from the world. It's a comfort issue. Most of the time I'd rather hang out with my family and close friends (most of whom are Christians) than befriend outsiders or serve strangers. Getting to know new people is uncomfortable. Reaching out to others means risking that they won't reach back. And here's the really bizarre part: I love talking about love! I get excited thinking about showing compassion to the needy and reaching out to my neighbors. But sometimes actually doing it is another matter. It's like the cartoon I saw of two friends reclining in a living room. One says to the other, "Of course I love people, in a theological sense."[4] Too often, that's me.

And I know I'm not alone. Many are quite happy to cordon themselves off in cozy Christian subcultures to avoid the risk and discomfort of interacting with outsiders. Yet you can't read the Gospels without seeing how contrary this is to what Jesus taught and modeled. Jesus was neck-deep in human needs. He touched people with disfiguring and contagious diseases. He washed his disciples' feet. He descended into the muck and mire of humanity. As his followers, we're called to do the same.

I'll be the first to acknowledge that this can be daunting. But it's okay to start small. The most encouraging advice

Mama Maggie gave during my interview with her was about what Western Christians can do to show God's love to the people around them:

> Jesus takes us always step by step. He doesn't reveal the whole all at once. Please take another step and do something to the closest person—inside your family, inside your town, inside your church. You can encourage someone with a word. You can give a flower to someone. You can do something. When you do, Jesus will open the door for you for more. Take the step.[5]

Hearing that advice was a relief to me. We don't have to become super-saints overnight. We just have to take one step, and then another one after that. It's a journey. And not one reserved for paid clergy or charity workers. We're all called to show the love of God to those far from him.

## INCARNATION

In 1976 Lesslie Newbigin retired as a missionary to South India and returned to his native England. But after a nearly forty-year absence, he found that his beloved homeland had changed dramatically. It was post-Christian. Newbigin concluded that England now needed the gospel as much as India. So instead of settling into a relaxing retirement, he began writing prolifically about how the church might communicate the gospel in an increasingly secular society.

Christians in the West had to start thinking like missionaries, he believed. All Christians were called to go to bring the gospel to their neighbors wherever they lived.[6] As a contemporary of Newbigin and fellow missionary Thomas Hale put it:

> There is no difference, in spiritual terms, between a missionary witnessing in his hometown and a missionary witnessing in Katmandu, Nepal. We are all called to go—even if it is only to the next room, or the next block.[7]

Talk of being a missionary in your neighborhood or being "missional" is now common language in Christian circles. That's in large part thanks to Newbigin. He introduced a radical shift in the way we think about our stance toward the culture. Like good missionaries, we must study our culture and live out the gospel in ways that are intelligible and compelling to our unbelieving neighbors.

Of course Newbigin's insight was nothing new. It was a rediscovery of ancient scriptural truth. The incarnation teaches us that love must be embodied. Eugene Peterson's artful rendering of John 1:14 described the incarnation of Jesus like this: "The Word became flesh and blood, / and moved into the neighborhood" (MSG).

When we ask how we can reach people far from God, we aren't asking anything new. God faced the problem ages ago. How could a sinless sovereign reach down in love to a fallen humanity?

The answer: he moved into our neighborhood. It wasn't a nice neighborhood. He didn't come for the upscale living and good schools. He moved into our neighborhood because he loved us.

In his last prayer on earth, Jesus made this request of his Father:

I do not ask that you take them out of the world, but that you keep them from the evil one. They are not of the world, just as I am not of the world. Sanctify them in the truth; your word is truth. As you sent me into the world, so I have sent them into the world. (John 17:15–18 ESV)

We are the living answers to that prayer. We remain in the world but are ever mindful that we are here on a mission; we've been sent. So we find creative and authentic ways to incarnate the gospel in a culture estranged from the principles of God's kingdom. We keep seeking out and loving people because we've been sought out and loved by God. We go anywhere people are because we have a God who was willing to go anywhere for us. We are other, yet intimate. Different from the world, yet immersed in it. Holy and loving—just like our Father.

## TIGER SIGHTING

We're always reduced to using metaphors when we talk about God, and this book started with an odd one.

I compared God to a tiger.

I hope that didn't offend you. My goal was to illustrate how dangerous and different from us God truly is.

Tigers are some of the most striking creatures on the planet. The sight of their vivid orange and black striping and lithe, muscular bodies produces a mixture of fascination and fear. Perhaps no one captured the essence of a tiger better than William Blake in his classic poem, "The Tyger." The first lines read:

*Tyger, tyger, burning bright,*
*In the forests of the night;*[8]

When we think of tigers, that's where we envision them—"in the forests of the night," or maybe stalking prey through the jungles of India. We imagine them wild. The reality, unfortunately, is not so idyllic. Tigers are in trouble. Over the past century the global tiger population has dropped by 97 percent. An estimated thirty-two hundred tigers remain in the wild, fewer than the number of captive tigers in the United States alone.[9] Today most tigers know nothing of dark forests and dense jungles. They live out their lives in cramped cement enclosures or chain-link cages. Most don't even know how to hunt. This apex predator, which for eons hunted vast territories and feared no natural enemy, no longer roams free. One of the most formidable animals in the world now slumbers behind safety glass while tourists file by to snap pictures.

The tiger has been tamed.

It's a tragedy that reminds me of another one: our attempts to tame a holy God.

God should command our highest loyalty and deepest reverence, yet often we try to domesticate him. Whether out of fear or pride or ignorance, we no longer appreciate his strangeness and splendor. We're not moved by his greatness and grandeur. We fail to tremble at his holiness. We avert our eyes from his brilliance. We spend our lives yawning at tigers.

Of course God will never suffer the fate of the tiger. We can do nothing to confine his power or reduce his majesty. As C. S. Lewis wrote, "A man can no more diminish God's glory by refusing to worship Him than a lunatic can put out the sun by scribbling the word, 'darkness' on the walls of his cell."[10] No, in our attempts to tame the Almighty, we succeed only in confining ourselves.

My hope is that you will break free. My prayer is that you will awaken to the awe of God, that you will open your life to his holiness and love. May he forever stalk your heart. May you learn to see his burning eyes amid the forests of your life.

# DISCUSSION GUIDE

**THIS GUIDE IS FAR MORE THAN A SET OF QUESTIONS TO** spark discussion, though it is that as well. It's designed to take a lofty subject—God's nature—and help you grapple with how you can apply these deep truths to your everyday life. A variety of people from business executives to stay-at-home moms chipped in to help create the questions and activities. The goal was to anticipate the ways in which the subject matter of the book can challenge, comfort, and stimulate change in your life. The discussion guide works equally well for small groups or individuals. Enjoy!

# CHAPTER 1: DIVINE INVASION

## DISCUSS

1. How is God like a lion? The Bible also describes God as a protective hen (Ps. 91:4). What do these images tell us about God's nature?

2. Would you describe your life with God as an adventure? Why or why not?

3. Does God's awesome power repel or draw you? Why? What does it mean to fear the Lord?

4. When do you glimpse God's greatness? While being in nature? Reading? Singing or listening to music? Participating in other activities?

5. How would gaining a greater appreciation for God's otherness affect your spiritual life?

## TAKE ACTION

Pop quiz! Fill in the blanks with the first thoughts that come to mind. (You will have an opportunity to retake the quiz at the end of the book to see how your view of God has evolved.)

1. When I think of God, the first word that comes to mind is _____.

2. When God looks at me, he sees _____.

3. _____ is the biggest obstacle in my spiritual life.

4. The characteristic of God that makes me most uncomfortable is _____.

5. The characteristic of God I find most comforting is _____.

6. Most of my friends would describe me as _____.

7. I believe my purpose is to _____.

8. _____ is crucial for an authentic
   relationship with God.

9. I feel energized to know God more intimately by
   _____.

10. I feel energized to love and serve those around me by
    _____.

## DIVE DEEPER
Read Psalm 29 every day this week.

- What is David's (the author) perspective of God in this psalm?
- Why do you think God's greatness and majesty is so important to David?
- Even after years of knowing God, why is David still in awe of God?

# CHAPTER 2: BEYOND THE SHALLOWS

## DISCUSS

1. Can you remember your first ocean experience? How old were you? What happened?
2. What are some of the factors that keep you in the shallows in your relationship with God? Are there aspects of your self-image you fear you might forfeit to follow God into the deep? Is there someone in your life who would feel threatened if you pursued a deeper relationship with God?

3. How do you respond when someone disrupts your sense of security and control? How important is your personal comfort? What effect does it have on your spiritual life?

4. What "man-made lagoons" can you identify in your spiritual life? Would you be willing to ask the Holy Spirit what they are?

5. Does the thought of totally surrendering your life to God excite or scare you? How would complete surrender affect your work and home life? How would it impact your relationships?

## TAKE ACTION

A friend once described the experience of living in Alaska during the dark winter months. "It was so cold and dark outside, I never felt fully awake," she said. I saw a spiritual parallel: many of us live only half awake to the reality of God. We sleepwalk through life, never fully alert to his grandeur and glory.

Identify some of the things that numb you to the awe of God. Are there distractions in your life that keep you from being spiritually awake? Is it work, busyness, technology, even church? Go outside at night at least once this week, and spend ten minutes looking at the night sky. Try to get a feel for the expanse of the universe and consider the magnitude of its Creator.

## DIVE DEEPER

Read Jeremiah 10.

• What are the main differences between idols and the true God in this chapter?

• What characteristics of God is Jeremiah trying to

illustrate with his description of nature in verses 12 and 13? Why do you think it's important to understand these attributes of God?

- Jeremiah asks God to discipline him, but "not in your anger" (v. 24). How might this kind of discipline be different from God's judgment? Would you ever ask God to discipline you?

## CHAPTER 3: THE GOD WORTH WORSHIPPING

### DISCUSS

1. Do you ever feel that a sense of God's greatness is missing from your worship experience? If so, why do you think that is?

2. Try to place yourself in Isaiah's position. If you had a vision of God like he did, how might you react? Would you welcome this kind of experience?

3. What are some of the ways we minimize God? Is there a tension between loving God and appreciating his holiness?

4. Are you ever struck by God's strangeness? What benefit could there be to realizing how different God is from us? How might you rediscover this dimension of God?

5. What is the relationship between understanding God's holiness and grasping his love? Why do we need a strange and holy God?

### TAKE ACTION

Find a sheet of paper and at the top of one side, write your name. On the opposite side, write "God." Under your name, list your characteristics. Write down words that describe you. They can be personality traits (outgoing, shy, dramatic) or words that describe humans in general (flawed, finite, spiritual). Under God's name, list attributes of God that come to mind. Think of the ways he's described in Scripture. After you've made it to the bottom of the page or can't think of any more words, stop and compare the lists. What are the differences? What attributes of God do you share? Are there characteristics of God that you could develop in your life?

## DIVE DEEPER

Read the poem below, written by the seventeenth-century theologian and hymn-writer Isaac Watts.

> ETERNAL POWER
> *Eternal Power, Whose high abode*
> *Becomes the grandeur of a God,*
> *Infinite lengths beyond the bounds*
> *Where stars resolve their little rounds!*
> *The lowest step around Thy seat,*
> *Rises too high for Gabriel's feet;*
> *In vain the favored angel tries*
> *To reach Thine height with wond'ring eyes.*
> *There while the first archangel sings,*
> *He hides his face behind his wings,*
> *And ranks of shining thrones around*
> *Fall worshiping, and spread the ground.*
> *Lord, what shall earth and ashes do?*
> *We would adore our Maker, too;*
> *From sin and dust to Thee we cry,*

*The Great, the Holy, and the High.*
*Earth from afar has heard Thy fame,*
*And worms have learned to lisp Thy Name;*
*But, O! the glories of Thy mind*
*Leave all our soaring thoughts behind.*
*God is in Heaven, and men below;*
*Be short our tunes, our words be few;*
*A solemn reverence checks our songs,*
*And praise sits silent on our tongues.*[1]

- How would you describe Watts's view of God?
- In Watts's view, what is the appropriate response of humans to a holy God?

## CHAPTER 4: A VISION OF HOLINESS

### DISCUSS

1. Have you sensed God's presence? If so, describe what your experiences were like.
2. How important is holiness in your life? Do you tend to see it as a burden or relief? Why?
3. Why do you think *holiness* has become a negative word? What are some of the misperceptions people have about holiness?
4. What does God's holiness teach you about your identity?
5. What feelings does a sense of God's holiness produce in you? How would a greater awareness of his holiness change your life?

## TAKE ACTION

For one day this week, try to keep a record of your sins. Include sinful thoughts and actions, sins of commission (the wrong things you do), and sins of omission (things you should do, but do not). Then the next day, record the good things you do. Again, examine both your thoughts and actions, good things you do, and temptations you resist.

Compare the records of the two days. How do your good deeds stack up against your sins? Which was more helpful: focusing on areas in which you fail or succeed? What did the exercise teach you about yourself and your need for grace?

## DIVE DEEPER

Read Philippians 2:1–17.

- What does this passage say about holiness?
- Is there one overriding virtue or quality in the kind of life Paul commanded the Philippians to lead?
- What does it mean that Jesus "made himself nothing" (v. 7) and "humbled himself" (v. 8)? How can you do that in your life?

## CHAPTER 5: DANGEROUS LIVING

## DISCUSS

1. How do you view the biblical descriptions of God's wrath in this chapter? What does God's wrath say about his character?

2. What realities do you discount or ignore in order to retain the comfort of order and predictability?

3. What emphasis did God place on safety and security in the design of creation? Is creation inherently safe and secure? What might this say about God?

4. What portion of your life focus (priorities, energy, time, resources) is directed toward ensuring current and future safety and security?

5. How can you live more dangerously for God right where you are?

## TAKE ACTION

Identify one thing you can do for someone else that will take you outside your comfort zone. It could be sharing your faith or helping a homeless person. But it could be as simple as giving cookies to your neighbor or expressing interest in a coworker's personal life. Whatever you decide to do, reflect on the experience afterward. Was it more or less difficult than you anticipated? Did God teach you anything through the experience? What might you do next that would help people even more and push you further outside your comfort zone?

## DIVE DEEPER

Read Acts 4.

- Why were Peter and John so fearless in proclaiming the message of Jesus?
- When they were threatened, what was their reaction?
- How would you have responded in the same situation?

- The authorities "took note that these men had been with Jesus" (v. 13). When people observe your actions, is it apparent that you've been with Jesus?

# CHAPTER 6: GOD INCOGNITO

## DISCUSS

1. Have you ever felt God's presence in an unlikely place? How can you be more alert to God's presence in the future?
2. Initially Carly typed two words: "hurt" and "help." What two words would you choose to describe yourself?
3. Why do you think Jesus was so understated about his identity?
4. Does God seem hidden to you? If so, why does God seem to hide?
5. The Bible says our true identities are "hidden with Christ" (Col. 3:3). What does this mean for how you understand yourself and how you relate to others?

## TAKE ACTION

In her book *The God Hunt*, Karen Mains encourages readers to record "God sightings." She described a God sighting as times when you experience:

- any obvious answer to prayer,
- any unexpected evidence of God's care,
- any help to do God's work, or
- any unusual linkage or timing.[2]

Using these guidelines, keep a journal for one week recording any God sightings. At the end of the week, reflect on what you learned. Were you surprised by how many (or how few) times you saw God at work in your life? What did the experience teach you about looking for evidence of God in your life and the world around you? What are some other ways God shows up in our lives?

## DIVE DEEPER
Read Acts 17:16–34.

- The passage records that Paul was "greatly distressed to see that the city [Athens] was full of idols" (v. 16). Name some of the biggest idols in our modern-day world.
- How about idols in your personal life? Which of these distress you the most?
- Paul also identified an Athenian altar dedicated "TO AN UNKNOWN GOD" (v. 23). What does this passage say about God's hiddenness?
- Why do you think Paul used a pagan altar to preach the gospel?
- What does this passage imply about the way God chooses to reveal himself?

## CHAPTER 7: LOVING A LION

## DISCUSS
1. Can you recall a time when you were overwhelmed by encountering a powerful animal or a natural wonder? What could such an experience teach you about God?

2. This chapter talks about two kinds of people: those who struggle to accept God's love, and those who struggle to accept his holiness. Which one are you?

3. Do you feel a tension between God's transcendence and immanence? If so, how do you react to that tension?

4. When you pray in private, what posture do you assume? Do you pray on your knees? Standing? Sitting down? Lying in bed? What might the postures of our bodies say about the way we approach God?

5. If you could see God in all his glory, how would that affect the way you view his love?

## TAKE ACTION

For the next three days, pray for at least ten minutes each day. During these prayer times, adopt a posture that conveys humility. If you're able, kneel on the floor or even lower your head to the ground. For the following three days, continue to pray for at least ten minutes each day, but change your posture. Position your body in a way that suggests confidence and gratitude. Perhaps it's standing with your arms raised or sitting with your head tilted toward the ceiling or sky. On the seventh day, reflect on the experience. Did the different prayer postures affect the content of your prayers? Did you learn anything about God? About yourself?

## DIVE DEEPER

Read Isaiah 40:9–31.

- How does this passage describe God?
- How do God's power and greatness relate to his love?
- What does God's power mean for his people?

# CHAPTER 8: TENACITY AND TENDERNESS

## DISCUSS

1. If you were in Hosea's position, how would you have responded to God's command to marry a prostitute? Why would God command him to do that?

2. What kind of things make God angry? Why do you think he so often relents from spilling out his wrath? Looking back at your life, are there times that make you particularly grateful for God's mercy?

3. Do you believe God has one perfect plan for you? Or does he have a plan B for your life?

4. Francis Thompson described God as "the Hound of Heaven," a relentless pursuer of the soul. Has that been your experience of God? In what ways do you feel he has pursued you relentlessly?

5. What are some of the things that keep you from feeling your need for God?

## TAKE ACTION

God told Hosea to marry a prostitute to represent Israel's unfaithfulness and God's unfailing love. Think of someone with whom you haven't gotten along. It doesn't have to be a sworn enemy, just someone who embarrasses or annoys you. Commit to doing a small act of kindness for that person this week. Afterward, reflect on the impact the act had on the person and on you. Write down names of other people to whom you could show kindness to express gratitude for the love God has shown for you.

## DIVE DEEPER

Read the first three chapters of Hosea.

- What do these chapters say about God?
- What do they say about Israel or humanity in general?
- When you think about God's tenacious love, what response do you have? Does it make you want to do something for God? For others?

# CHAPTER 9: INTIMATE BEGINNINGS

## DISCUSS

1. What kind of feelings does the picture of Jesus face-to-face with the Father stir in you? How does it affect your view of God?
2. What does the intimacy Jesus had with the Father mean for your relationship with God?
3. Jesus addressed God with *Abba*, a term of intimacy and respect. What names do you use? What might they suggest about your view of him?
4. Do you find the idea of Jesus' humanity and physicality disturbing or comforting? Why?
5. Have you ever been simultaneously struck by a sense of both God's greatness and his love? Or is it usually only one or the other? Why?

## TAKE ACTION

One of the spiritual practices described by St. Ignatius

Loyola is what he called "the contemplation on the love of God." It involves reflecting on four themes:

1. God's gifts to us (life, family, friends, faith, church, eternal life),
2. God's self-giving in Jesus,
3. God's continuing work in the world, and
4. the limitless quality of God's love.[3]

Incorporate these four themes into your prayers this week. At the conclusion of your prayer times, end by reciting a prayer penned by St. Ignatius:

Take, Lord, and receive all my liberty, my memory, my understanding, and my entire will—all that I have and call my own. You have given it all to me. To you, Lord, I return it. Everything is yours; do with it what you will. Give me only your love and your grace. That is enough for me.[4]

## DIVE DEEPER
Read John 1.

- List the various ways Jesus is described in this chapter.
- Which images do you find particularly interesting? Are any confusing?
- What do you believe John was trying to convey with these descriptions?

## CHAPTER 10: FACE-TO-FACE

### DISCUSS

1. What does it mean to you that the temple curtain was torn when Jesus died?
2. What do you feel is more needed in your life: knowledge of God or experiences of him? How do the two relate?
3. Since the barriers between God and us have been removed, what role should holiness play in our lives? How can you be a dwelling place for the Lord?
4. Are there experiences, mind-sets, or false beliefs that interfere with your accepting God's love?
5. In what ways does our world work against our ability to rest in God's love? What will it take to see yourself as a beloved child of your Father in heaven?

### TAKE ACTION

Spend fifteen minutes in prayer each day this week. At the end of each prayer time, imagine standing in the temple. The thick curtain sectioning off the Holy of Holies is directly in front of you. Picture the curtain being torn and falling to the ground. Imagine yourself walking over the torn curtain and into the Holy of Holies. Once you can imagine yourself in the Holy of Holies, kneel down and spend some time being in God's presence.

### DIVE DEEPER

Read 1 Kings 6, which describes the construction of the first Jewish temple built by King Solomon.

Then take a tour of the second Jewish temple. Well, take a

virtual one at least. Go to: Jerusalem.com/tour/jewish_temple
_3D/web. This virtual tour will give you a glimpse at what the
temple might have looked like at the time of Christ.

After reading 1 Kings 6 and taking the virtual 3D tour of
the second temple, answer these questions:

- Why do you think such precise dimensions and
  instructions were given for the construction of Solomon's
  temple? And why did it have to be a lavish and beautiful
  building?
- What does the temple's grandeur say about the worship
  of God?
- What does the Bible mean when it calls our bodies the
  temple of the Holy Spirit?

## CHAPTER 11: JESUS IN THE SHADOWS

### DISCUSS

1. Have you experienced a season of suffering in your life?
   What did the suffering of Jesus mean to you during that
   time? What about now as you look back on it?
2. Does the image of a suffering Messiah trouble or
   comfort you? Why?
3. Why do you think Jesus cried, "My God, my God, why
   have you forsaken me?" from the cross (Mark 15:34)?
   Have you ever felt forsaken by God?
4. Why does God allow suffering? When you suffer,
   would you rather have someone to tell you why you're
   suffering—or someone to try to understand your pain?

5. Have you ever felt Jesus' presence in the midst of pain or loss? What assurances can you provide for others when they suffer?

## TAKE ACTION

This week, reach out to someone who is suffering. It could be someone who is battling a health crisis, who has just lost a loved one, or who is experiencing a family crisis. Contact the person and ask how he or she is doing and just listen. Try not to give him or her answers or fix his or her problems. Instead thank him or her for sharing what he or she's going through, offer your sympathy, and say you'll pray that he or she would feel Christ's presence in the midst of his or her trial.

## DIVE DEEPER

Read Mark 14:32–42, the account of Jesus in the Garden of Gethsemane.

- Does anything surprise you about this story?
- What does Jesus' prayer reveal about his relationship with the Father?
- How can the way Jesus faced death help you when you suffer?

## CHAPTER 12: THE FRAGRANCE OF ETERNITY

## DISCUSS

1. Have you met someone in whom you sensed God's presence? What was it about this person that gave you

that impression?

2. When it comes to the outside culture, is your instinct to withdraw or engage? What is a healthy balance between being in the world, but not of it?

3. How can you model God's otherness when it comes to relating to others outside the church? How about his intimacy?

4. Why do you think Christians so often get stuck in holy huddles, lobbing "truth grenades" at the outside world? How can the incarnation help free us from this isolation?

5. What can you do to encourage fellow believers to be more active in modeling truth and love together?

## TAKE ACTION

Remember the pop quiz you took after reading chapter 1? Without looking back at the results, take it again. Fill in the blanks with the first thoughts that come to mind.

1. When I think of God, the first word that comes to mind is _____.

2. When God looks at me, he sees _____.

3. _____ is the biggest obstacle in my spiritual life.

4. The characteristic of God that makes me most uncomfortable is _____.

5. The characteristic of God I find most comforting is

_____.

6. Most of my friends would describe me as

_____.

7. I believe my purpose is to _____.

8. _____ is crucial for an authentic relationship with God.

9. I feel energized to know God more intimately by _____.

10. I feel energized to love and serve those around me by

_____.

Now that you've completed it, compare the second quiz to your first one. Were any of your answers different? If so, what do you think those changes say about the way your view of God is changing?

## DIVE DEEPER

Read the following passage from Dietrich Bonhoeffer's book *Life Together:*

> Jesus Christ lived in the midst of his enemies. At the end all his disciples deserted him. On the Cross he was utterly alone, surrounded by evildoers and mockers. For this cause he had come, to bring peace to the enemies of God. So the Christian, too, belongs not in the seclusion of a cloistered life but in the thick of foes. There is his commission, his work.[5]

In what ways have you opted for enjoying personal comfort over bringing peace to the enemies of God? How can you follow Jesus' example of loving others even in the midst of your enemies?

# ACKNOWLEDGMENTS

**THIS BOOK WAS A STRUGGLE.**

In the past, I've written mainly about ministry trends and topics. I quickly learned that writing about God is far different. Never have I felt so out of my depth. Never have my own resources—spiritual and intellectual—been so clearly unequal to a task.

I couldn't have done it alone. The following people offered their wisdom, support, and encouragement. It hasn't gone unnoticed.

Thanks to . . .

The Thomas Nelson team: Joel Miller, for believing in the book and refining it with your keen editorial and theological insights. Heather Skelton and Jennifer Stair, for giving the manuscript those crucial final touches.

Marshall Allen: mentor, friend, agent, and journalist extraordinaire. I'm grateful for your friendship. Thanks for the hours of conversation about the book and all the encouragement along the way.

Writer friends: Brandon O'Brien, Skye Jethani, Kevin Miller, Matt Woodley, Marshall Shelley, Doug and Angie Franklin, Amy Simpson, David Kopp, Matthew Lee Anderson, John Dickerson, Daniel Darling, Sam O'Neal, Paul Pastor, Kevin Emmert, Kyle Rohane, John Wilson, and Jason Johansen—you're all great friends and superb writers. Your input was invaluable.

My neighbor, Dave: for raiding my bookshelf, and then returning the books with the best passages underlined.

The fam: My parents (Art and Margee) and brothers (Dan, Darren, Dave) and Grandpa (Merle) for all your love and support. The Keohanes, my second family, for letting me marry your daughter, and putting up with me ever since. Jason and Faith, Nathanael and Kerri and Cory. Thanks for your thoughtful contributions to the Discussion Guide.

Grace: My ethereal wife of 11 years. You constantly amaze me with your kindness, intelligence, and gentle wisdom. Every day I thank God you're in my life.

God: When the veil is lifted, I will say with Job, "Surely I spoke of things I did not understand, / things too wonderful for me to know" (42:3). Until then, I'll pray with David, "May the words of my mouth and the meditation of my heart be acceptable in your sight, O LORD" (Ps. 19:14).

# NOTES

## CHAPTER 1: DIVINE INVASION

1. Oswald Chambers, quoted in Martin H. Manser, ed. *The Westminster Collection of Christian Quotations* (Louisville: Westminster John Knox Press, 2001), 131.

2. Ibid.

3. Christina Caron, "Zanesville Animal Massacre Included 18 Rare Bengal Tigers," *ABC News*, October 19, 2011, http://abcnews.go.com/US/zanesville-animal-massacre-included-18-rare-bengal-tigers/story?id=14767017.

4. See, for example, the following verses: "For the LORD your God is *a consuming fire*" (Deut. 4:24); "Will not the *Judge of all the earth* do right?" (Gen. 18:25); "The LORD *of hosts*, he is the King of glory!" (Ps. 24:10 ESV).

5. See, for example, "God is not human, that he should lie, not a human being, that he should change his mind" (Num. 23:19).

6. Carl Grossman, "Brighter Than the Brightest Star," *Learning*

*to Glow: A Nuclear Reader*, ed. John Bradley (The University of Arizona Press, 2000), 190.

7. Phred Dvorak, "Japanese Nuclear Cleanup Workers Detail Lax Safety Practices at Plant," *The Wall Street Journal, June 14, 2011*, http://online.wsj.com/article/SB1000142405270230490600457 6371300261616120.html.

8. Danielle Dauenhauer, "13 Idiots Who Climbed the Fence at the Zoo," *Ranker*, http://www.ranker.com/list/13-of-the-best -idiots-climbing-the-wall-at-the-zoo/danielle-dauenhauer.

9. Eugene Peterson, *Leap over a Wall* (New York: HarperOne, 1998), 144.

10. Ibid.

11. Annie Dillard, *Teaching a Stone to Talk* (New York: HarperCollins, 1982), 52.

12. Kevin Miller, "The Fear of God" (sermon, Church of the Resurrection, Wheaton, IL), October 2007, http://www .preachingtoday.com/sermons/outlines/2007/october /fearofgod.html.

## CHAPTER 2: BEYOND THE SHALLOWS

1. Origen, *Homilies on Genesis and Exodus*, trans. Ronald E. Heine, Fathers of the Church Series, vol. 71 (Washington, DC: The Catholic University of America Press, 1982).

2. John Calvin, *Commentaries on the Four Last Books of Moses Arranged in the Form of a Harmony*, trans. C. W. Bingham (Bellingham, WA: Logos Bible Software, 2010), Exodus 32:1.

3. Eusebius of Caesarea, *Against Paganism*, ed. Aryeh Kofsky (Amherst, NY: Humanities Press, 2001), 110.

4. Donald McCullough, *The Trivialization of God: The Dangerous Illusion of a Manageable Deity* (Colorado Springs: NavPress, 1995).

5. Hilton Waikoloa, "Pools and Beach," http://www
.hiltonwaikoloavillage.com/pools_and_beach/beach_and
_lagoon.cfm.

6. Henry David Thoreau, *Walden* (1854), chapter 1.

7. John Blase, "That's the Deep," *A Deeper Church* (blog), October
26, 2012, http://deeperstory.com/thats-the-deep/.

8. *Environmental News Service*, "Diversity, Beauty of Marine Life
Charted in First Global Census," October 5, 2010; *The Week*,
"Ocean Life, Fathomed," October 22, 2010, 26.

9. Margaret Feinberg, *Wonderstruck: Awaken to the Nearness of God*
(Nashville: Worthy Publishing, 2012), 27.

## CHAPTER 3: THE GOD WORTH WORSHIPPING

1. Matt Chandler, *The Explicit Gospel* (Wheaton, IL: Crossway,
2012), 21.

2. Ronald F. Youngblood, F. F. Bruce, and R. K. Harrison, eds.,
*Compact Bible Dictionary* (Nashville: Thomas Nelson, 2004), 558.

3. R. C. Sproul, *The Holiness of God* (Carol Stream, IL: Tyndale,
1985), 43.

4. Rudolf Otto, *The Idea of the Holy,* full text available at http://
archive.org/stream/theideaoftheholy00ottouoft
/theideaoftheholy00ottouoft_djvu.txt.

5. Anne Lamott, *Help, Thanks, Wow: The Three Essential Prayers*
(New York: Riverhead, 2012), 2.

6. Jud Wilhite, *Pursued: God's Divine Obsession with You* (Nashville:
FaithWords, 2013).

7. Thomas E. Bergler, "When Are We Going to Grow Up? The
Juvenilization of American Christianity," *Christianity Today*,
June 8, 2012, http://www.christianitytoday.com/ct/2012/june
/when-are-we-going-to-grow-up.html.

8. Lillian Daniel, "The Church Calendar: New and Improved," *Huffington Post* (blog), February 5, 2013, http://www .huffingtonpost.com/lillian-daniel/the-church-calendar-new -a_b_2600258.html.

9. William Paul Young, *The Shack* (Newbury Park, CA: Windblown Media, 2007).

10. *Merriam-Webster,* Merriam-Webster.com, s.v. "expert."

11. Gregory of Nyssa, *Homilies on Ecclesiastes 7,* quoted in Kallistos Ware, *The Orthodox Way* (Crestwood, NY: St. Vladimir's Seminary Press, 1995), 24.

12. C. S. Lewis, *A Grief Observed* (London: Faber & Faber, 1961), 52.

13. Victor White, *God, the Unknown, and Other Essays* (New York: Harper, 1956), 23–24.

14. Jonathan Culler, *Literary Criticism: A Very Short Introduction* (Oxford University Press, 2000), 79.

15. John Koessler, *Folly, Grace, and Power: The Mysterious Act of Preaching* (Grand Rapids: Zondervan, 2011), 98.

## CHAPTER 4: A VISION OF HOLINESS

1. James Hampton, *The Throne of the Third Heaven of the Nations' Millennium General Assembly,* Exhibition Label, Smithsonian American Art Museum, 2006, http://americanart.si.edu /collections/search/artwork/?id=9897.

2. Kevin DeYoung, *The Hole in Our Holiness: Filling the Gap between Gospel, Passion, and the Pursuit of Godliness* (Wheaton, IL: Crossway, 2012), 11.

3. The Barna Group, "The Concept of Holiness Baffles Most Americans," February 20, 2006, http://www.barna.org/barna -update/article/5-barna-update/162-the-concept-of-holiness -baffles-most-americans.

4. *Strong's Exhaustive Concordance,* 75 s.v. *agonizomai:* The

Greek word translated "strive" is *agonizomai*, and it implies an agonizing, intense, purposeful struggle.

5. Tyler Braun, "What We've Lost Does Not Outweigh What We Can Gain," *Man of Depravity* (blog), September 2012, http://manofdepravity.com/2012/09/loss-gain/.

6. Brett McCracken, "Have Christians Lost Their Sense of Difference?" *Mere Orthodoxy* (blog), June 19, 2013, http://mereorthodoxy.com/have-christians-lost-their-sense-of-difference/.

7. Tyler Braun, "A Better Formula," *Man of Depravity* (blog), September 28, 2012, http://manofdepravity.com/2012/09/a-better-formula/.

8. Lesslie Newbigin, *Proper Confidence: Faith, Doubt, and Certainty in Christian Discipleship* (Grand Rapids: Eerdmans, 1995), 88.

9. Tyler Braun, "What We've Lost Does Not Outweigh What We Can Gain." *Man of Depravity* (blog), September 2012, http://manofdepravity.com/2012/09/loss-gain/.

10. David F. Wright, Sinclair B. Ferguson, and J. I. Packer, eds., *New Dictionary of Theology* (Downers Grove, IL: IVP Academic, 1988), 271.

11. Bill Giovannetti, "Great Worship with Modest Means," *Leadership Journal*, vol. 15, no. 2 (Spring 1994), http://www.christianitytoday.com/le/1994/spring/4l2052.html.

12. Matt Redman, *Facedown* (New York: Regal, 2004), 23.

13. John Eldredge, *The Utter Relief of Holiness* (Nashville: FaithWords, 2013).

14. *Holy Bible Dictionary*, 273.

15. Louis Berkhof, *Systematic Theology* (Grand Rapids: Eerdmans, 1938), 527.

16. Louis Berkhof, *Manual of Christian Doctrine* (Grand Rapids: Eerdmans, 1939), 24.

17. Marva J. Dawn, *Reaching Out Without Dumbing Down* (Grand Rapids: Eerdmans, 1995), 98–99.

## CHAPTER 5: DANGEROUS LIVING

1. Mary Louise Bringle, "Debating Hymns," *The Christian Century*, May 1, 2013, http://www.christiancentury.org/article /2013-04/debating-hymns.

2. Miroslav Volf, *Free of Charge* (Grand Rapids: Zondervan, 2006), 138–39.

3. The fear of the Lord teaches one wisdom (Prov. 15:33); the fear of the Lord is the beginning of knowledge (Prov. 1:7); the fear of the Lord lengthens life (Prov. 10:27).

4. John Piper, *The Pleasures of God* (Colorado Springs: Multnomah, 1991), 205–6.

5. US Department of Homeland Security, *Budget-in Brief: Fiscal Year 2012*, http://www.dhs.gov/xlibrary/assets/budget-bib -fy2012.pdf.

6. "Seven Questions for New Converts in an Asian Country," *Preaching Today*, February 2012, http://www.preachingtoday .com/illustrations/2012/february/2021312.html.

7. John R. W. Stott, *The Message of 1 Timothy and Titus*, Bible Speaks Today (Downers Grove, IL: IVP Academic, 2001).

8. Tim Challies, "That God Would Make Us Dangerous," November 20, 2011, http://www.challies.com/quotes/that-god -would-make-us-dangerous.

9. Rodney Stark, *The Rise of Christianity: How the Obscure, Marginal Jesus Movement Became the Dominant Religious Force in the Western World in a Few Centuries* (San Francisco: Harper Collins, 1997).

10. *Eusebius's Ecclesiastical History* (New York: Merchant Books, 2011), 9.8.13-14.

11. "Africa: Christians outnumber Muslims," *Vatican Insider*, September 21, 2012, http://vaticaninsider.lastampa.it/en/ documents/detail/articolo/africa-africa-18309/.

12. Thomas Chalmers, "The Expulsive Power of a New Affection," (sermon), date unknown, www.theologynetwork.org.

13. Nicole Yorio and Lindsey Palmer, "The Truth about Why Men Cheat," NBCNews.com, *Today Health*, October 17, 2008, http://www.today.com/id/27223225/ns/today-today_health/t/truth-about-why-men-cheat/.

14. Connie Jakab, *Culture Rebel* (Bloomington, IN: WestBow Press, 2012), 24.

15. Mark Buchanan, "It's Your Call," *Leadership Journal*, vol. 34, no. 1 (Winter 2013), http://www.christianitytoday.com/le/2013/winter/its-your-call.html?start=1.

16. Joseph Loconte, *The Searchers: A Quest for Faith in the Valley of Doubt* (Nashville: Thomas Nelson, 2012), 2–3.

17. CNN Staff, "Chinese Zoo Angers Visitors by Passing Off Hairy Tibetan Mastiff Dog as Lion," CNN.com, August 16, 2013, http://www.cnn.com/2013/08/16/world/asia/china-zoo-dog-lion/index.html.

## CHAPTER 6: GOD INCOGNITO

1. James D. Weatherly, "You're the Best Thing That Ever Happened to Me," sung by Ray Price, lyrics available at http://www.metrolyrics.com/youre-the-best-thing-that-ever-happened-to-me-lyrics-price-ray.html.

2. R. Kelly, "I Believe I Can Fly" by Robert S. Kelly and Catherine Sadok, recorded 2003 on *The R. in R&B Collection*, lyrics available at http://metrolyrics.com/i-believe-i-can-fly-lyrics-r-kelly.html.

3. Ibid.

4. C. S. Lewis, *Letters to Malcolm: Chiefly on Prayer* (Fort Washington, PA: Harvest Books, 1964), 44.

5. Alan B. Goldberg and Lauren Putrino, "Teen Locked in Autistic Body Finds Inner Voice," ABC, *20/20*, June 6, 2009.

6. Malcolm Muggeridge, *A Third Testament* (Maryknoll, NY: Orbis, 2004), 70.

7. Philip Yancey, *The Jesus I Never Knew* (Grand Rapids: Zondervan, 1995), 21.

8. *Undercover Boss*, season 1, episode 3, "7-Eleven," February 21, 2010.

## CHAPTER 7: LOVING A LION

1. "Immanent," Theopedia, http://www.theopedia.com/Immanence _of_God."

2. Apophatic theology was first developed by Jewish and Christian thinkers, and adopted in the Middle Ages by Islamic scholars. Yet this "negative theology," or *lahoot salbi*, is prominent in Islamic thought to this day.

3. John Garrett, *A Classical Dictionary of India: Illustrative of the Mythology, Philosophy, Literature, Antiquities, Arts, Manners, Customs of the Hindus* (Ulan Press, 2012), 102.

4. Steven Boyer and Christopher Hall, *The Mystery of God: Theology for Knowing the Unknowable* (Ada, MI: Baker Academic, 2013), 23.

5. A. W. Tozer, *The Knowledge of the Holy* (San Francisco: Harper and Row, 1961), 80.

6. N. Sarna, *Exploring Exodus: The Origins of Biblical Israel* (New York: Schocken Books, 1996), 52.

7. Michael P. Knowles, *The Unfolding Mystery of the Divine Name: The God of Sinai in Our Midst* (Downers Grove, IL: InterVarsity, 2012), 32–33.

8. Ibid., 34.

9. Francis Chan, *Crazy Love: Overwhelmed by a Relentless God* (Colorado Springs: David C. Cook, 2008), 59.

10. Sam Storms, "The Holiness of God," *Enjoying God* (blog), May

6, 2006, http://www.samstorms.com/all-articles/post/the
-holiness-of-god/.

11. Philip Yancey, *The Jesus I Never Knew* (Grand Rapids:
Zondervan, 1995), 38–39.

## CHAPTER 8: TENACITY AND TENDERNESS

1. *Strong's Exhaustive Concordance,* s.v. *zânûwn,* 2183.

2. Luc Besson, Robert Mark Kamen, *Taken*, 20th Century Fox,
September 19, 2008.

3. Lesslie Newbigin, quoted in Krish Kandiah, "The Missionary
Who Wouldn't Retire," *Christianity Today*, December 8, 2009,
http://www.christianitytoday.com/ct/2010/january/1.44.html.

4. Francis Thompson, "The Hound of Heaven," in Nicholson
& Lee, eds., *The Oxford Book of English Mystical Verse* (Oxford
University Press, 1917), http://www.bartleby.com/236/239.html.

5. Ibid.

6. C. S. Lewis, *Surprised by Joy: The Shape of my Early Life* (New
York: Harcourt, 1966), 228.

7. Marguerite Shuster, *The Fall and Sin* (Grand Rapids: Eerdmans,
2003), 164.

8. Tom Brady, "Tom Brady on Fears," interview on *60 Minutes*,
December 23, 2007, http://www.cbsnews.com/video/watch
/?id=1015829n.

9. Saint Augustine, *Confessions* (New York: Simon & Shuster, 2012
ed.), 3.

10. Steve Salerno, *Sham: How the Self-Help Movement Made America
Helpless* (New York: Random House, 2005), 24–25.

11. Brennan Manning, *The Ragamuffin Gospel: Good News for
the Bedraggled, Beat-Up, and Burnt Out* (Colorado Springs:
Multnomah, 2005), 49.

12. Nikolas Warwickshire, "Liberal Christianity, Homosexuality,

and the Love of Scripture," *Scribbles of a Sporadic Scribe* (blog), July 6, 2013, http://scribblesofasporadicscribe.wordpress. com/2013/07/06/liberal-christianity-homosexuality-and-the -love-of-scripture-the-problem-with-assuming-any-christian -group-loves-or-hates-the-bible/.

## CHAPTER 9: INTIMATE BEGINNINGS

1. Sinclair B. Ferguson and David F. Wright, eds., *New Dictionary of Theology* (Downers Grove, IL: InterVarsity, 1988), 395.

2. *Strong's Exhaustive Concordance* 4314, s.v. pros. The preposition *pros* means "toward" or "facing."

3. Fr. Patrick Henry Reardon, "Daily Reflections," *Touchstone Magazine,* June 8, 2003, http://www.touchstonemag.com/frpat /2003_06_01_frpatarchive.html.

4. *Strong's Exhaustive Concordance,* 4561, s.v. *sarx,* referencing the base of 4563, *saroo,* http://biblesuite.com/greek/4561.htm.

5. William D. Mounce, *The Basics of Biblical Greek* (Grand Rapids: Zondervan, 2009), 75.

6. JewishEncyclopedia.com, "Moses," http://www.jewishencyclopedia .com/articles/11049-moses.

7. Eric Bazilian, "What If God Was One of Us?" performed by Joan Osborne on *Relish,* released March 1995.

8. In the New Testament, Abba is typically followed by the Greek word, *pater,* which is not the Greek word for Daddy. The Greek language has a word for "Daddy"—*pappas*—but that is not the word the New Testament uses to translate Abba. For more, see Shane Lems, "'Abba' Is Not 'Daddy,'" The Aquila Report, January 9, 2013, http://theaquilareport.com/abba-is-not-daddy/.

9. J. N. Andrews, *The Complete Testimony of the Fathers,* 31–32, http://sdapillars.org/media/EGWattitudesinPrayer.pdf.

10. A photograph is found in C. K. Barrett, *The Pastoral Epistles*, New Clarendon Bible series (Oxford: Clarendon Press, 1968), 53.

11. R. C. Sproul, *The Holiness of God* (Wheaton, IL: Tyndale, 1985), 22.

## CHAPTER 10: FACE-TO-FACE

1. William Shakespeare, *Romeo and Juliet*, Act V, Scene 3, line 322.

2. Most translations of this utterance read, "Surely this man was the son of God." But there is no definite article before God in the original Greek text. The original Revised Standard Version reads, "Surely this man was the son of a god" (RSV). This is probably a better reading. Since the centurion was most likely polytheistic (and not a monotheistic Jew), it would make sense for him to attribute the strange phenomenon to Jesus being the son of a god, rather than the Son of God.

3. English translation by Jacob Neusner, *The Talmud of the Land of Israel: An Academic Commentary to the Second, Third and Fourth Divisions*, IV. *Yerushalmi Tractate Yoma*, South Florida Academic Commentary Series 112 (Atlanta: Scholars Press, 1998), 148.

4. Jonathan Martin, *Prototype: What Happens When You Discover You're More Like Jesus Than You Think?* (Wheaton, IL: Tyndale, 2013), 22.

5. Babylonian Talmud, Baba Batra, 4a; Shemot Rabba 36:1.

6. Thomas Aquinas, quoted in *The Oxford Dictionary of the Christian Church*, 3rd ed. (New York: Oxford University Press, 1997), 1615.

7. J. I. Packer, *Knowing God* (Downers Grove, IL: InterVarsity, 1993).

## CHAPTER 11: JESUS IN THE SHADOWS

1. James Stewart, *A Faith to Proclaim* (Vancouver, BC: Regent College Publishing, 2002), 102.

2. The very word *compassion* comes from the Latin *compassio*, which literally means "to suffer with."

3. Jürgen Moltmann, *The Crucified God* (Minneapolis: First Fortress Press, 1993), 201.

4. Christian Wiman, *My Bright Abyss* (New York: Farrar, Straus and Giroux, 2013), 30.

5. Ibid., 155.

6. Ed Stetzer, "Dirty God: An Interview with Johnnie Moore," *The Exchange* (blog), *Christianity Today*, May 7, 2013, http://www.christianitytoday.com/edstetzer/2013/may/dirty-god-interview-with-johnnie-moore.html.

7. Richard Wurmbrand, *Preparing for the Underground Church* (Bartlesville, OK: Voice of the Martyrs, 2010), http://preparingfortheundergroundchurchbook.blogspot.com.

8. Ajith Fernando, *The Call to Joy and Pain* (Wheaton, IL: Crossway, 2007), 51–52.

## CHAPTER 12: THE FRAGRANCE OF ETERNITY

1. Marshall Shelley, "The Fire Within Mama Maggie," *Leadership Journal*, Fall 2011, http://www.christianitytoday.com/le/2011/fall/mamamaggie.html.

2. St. Teresa of Avila, *Interior Castle* (Mineola, NY: Dover, 1946), 23.

3. "Truth Bombs Versus an Incarnational Truth," http://www.preachingtoday.com/illustrations/2008/october/2101308.html.

4. Lee D. Johnson, "Love, Theologically Speaking," http://www.buildingchurchleaders.com/multimedia/cartoons/14914.html.

5. Marshall Shelley, "The Fire Within Mama Maggie," *Leadership Journal*, Fall 2011, http://www.christianitytoday.com/le/2011/fall/mamamaggie.html.

6. Lesslie Newbigin, *The Gospel in a Pluralist Society* (Grand Rapids: Eerdmans, 1989), 230.

7. Thomas Hale, *On Being a Missionary* (Pasadena, CA: William Carey Library Publishers, 2003), 6.

8. William Blake, "The Tiger," in Arthur Quiller-Couch, ed., The *Oxford Book of English Verse: 1250–1900* (Oxford: Oxford University Press, 1919), http://www.bartleby.com/101/489.html.

9. "Facts about Tigers," wwf.panda.org./what_we_do/ endangered_species/tigers/about_tigers/.

10. C. S. Lewis, *The Problem of Pain* (New York: HarperCollins, 1996), 46–47.

## DISCUSSION GUIDE

1. Isaac Watts, "Eternal Power," *Horae Lyricae* (London: S. and D. Bridge, 1706).

2. Karen Mains, *The God Hunt: The Delightful Chase and the Wonder of Being Found* (Downers Grove, IL: InterVarsity, 2003).

3. St. Ignatius Loyola, "Contemplation on the Love of God," *Spiritual Exercises*, 231–37, http://www.ignatianspirituality.com /ignatian-prayer/the-spiritual-exercises/contemplation-on-the -love-of-god/.

4. Ibid.

5. Dietrich Bonhoeffer, *Life Together: The Classic Exploration of Faith in Community* (New York: Harper & Row, 1954).

# ABOUT THE AUTHOR

**DREW NATHAN DYCK (M.A. IN THEOLOGY) IS MANAGING EDITOR** of *Leadership Journal* and the author of *Generation Ex-Christian: Why Young Adults Are Leaving the Faith . . . And How to Bring Them Back* (Moody). Drew's work has appeared in numerous publications including *USA Today*, *The Huffington Post*, *Relevant*, and *Christianity Today*. He lives with his wife, Grace, and son, Athanasius, in the Chicago area. They attend Church of the Resurrection in Wheaton, Illinois. Connect with Drew at DrewDyck.com or follow him on Twitter @drewdyck.

"Drew Dyck possesses a skill for seeing connections between everyday experiences and spiritual reality. This book made me long for further encounters with the untamed God."

KATHRYN CALLAHAN-HOWELL, PASTOR, WINTON COMMUNITY FREE METHODIST CHURCH, CINCINNATI, OHIO

"Lively, provocative, and made me want to pray. Read it, and you may find yourself falling to your knees."

KEVIN MILLER, EDITOR-AT-LARGE, *Leadership Journal*

"Drew Dyck articulates the man-centered obsession of the Western church and calls us to bow in reverence and awe at God's breathtaking holiness and love."

SCOTT THOMAS, FORMER DIRECTOR, ACTS 29 NETWORK

"*Yawning at Tigers* reminds us that we are made for so much more than service as shabby idols for self-worship."

AMY SIMPSON, EDITOR, GIFTEDFORLEADERSHIP.COM; AUTHOR, *Troubled Minds: Mental Illness and the Church's Mission*

"Drew Dyck shows that the holiness of God reveals our smallness and God's bigness, our imperfections and God's perfections. We have to be reminded that we are not God before we cry out for God's help. Thank you, Drew, for reminding me of this. I keep forgetting."

TULLIAN TCHIVIDJIAN, PASTOR, CORAL RIDGE PRESBYTERIAN CHURCH; AUTHOR, *One Way Love: Inexhaustible Grace for an Exhausted World.*

"With clear prose and dynamic stories, Dyck shows us the way to a deeper understanding of the life that awaits us, one that until now we have been too afraid to live. The only question is, 'Are you ready for some danger?'"

JIM BELCHER, ASSOCIATE PROFESSOR OF PRACTICAL THEOLOGY, KNOX THEOLOGICAL SEMINARY; AUTHOR, *In Search of Deep Faith: A Pilgrimage into the Beauty, Goodness, and Heart of Christianity.*

# PRAISE FOR ~~WITHDRAWN~~

"*Yawning at Tigers* is a needed corrective to self-indulgent Christianity. I hope people listen."

PHILIP YANCEY, AUTHOR, *The Jesus I Never Knew*

"Convicting, compelling, creative—here's a stirring challenge to experience God in all his awesome glory and breathtaking grace! Invite our holy and loving God to roam freely in your life."

LEE STROBEL, AUTHOR, *The Case for Christ.*

"From the beginning we've been casting God in our image. But he cannot be tamed by our timid imaginations. Drew Dyck will take you to God's Word so you can see the Father, Son, and Holy Spirit as utterly holy and perfectly loving."

COLLIN HANSEN, AUTHOR, *Young, Restless, Reformed*

"Drew Dyck challenges the reader to revere God as he truly is: impressive, weighty, and holy. Dyck deftly weaves together modern illustrations with scriptural insight to paint a powerful picture of a loving and powerful God and Father."

ED STETZER, PRESIDENT, LIFEWAY RESEARCH

"Thin notions of God's transcendence are undermining the church's vitality and witness to the world. *Yawning at Tigers* is a strong antidote against a domesticated God."

MATTHEW LEE ANDERSON, MEREORTHODOXY.COM

"*Yawning at Tigers* is a sharp diagnosis of the church's cavalier attitude toward God and a fervent and winsome call to rediscover God's beautiful, terrible holiness."

MARK BUCHANAN, AUTHOR, *Your Church is Too Safe*

"This book will inspire many to pursue God with courage."

J. LEE GRADY, FORMER EDITOR, *Charisma*